Christina Costanza

IT'S JUST MY NATURE!

A GUIDE TO KNOWING AND LIVING YOUR TRUE NATURE

CAROL TUTTLE

Bestselling author of *Remembering Wholeness*

LIVE YOUR TRUTH
PRESS

Printed in the United States of America
Second Edition
17 18 19 20 10 9 8 7

Dressing Your Truth®, Beauty Profiling℠, Energy Profiling®, Body Profiling℠, Energy Type℠, Energy Draping℠, and TYPE 1℠, TYPE 2℠, TYPE 3℠, and TYPE 4℠ are trademarks or registered trademarks of Carol Tuttle Enterprises, LLC.

ISBN: 978-0-9785436-9-3
Library of Congress Card Catalogue No.: 2009925814

Cover and text design by Beth Farrell
Text layout by Tara Mayberry
Book cover photo by Debra Macfarlane
www.debramacfarlane.com

LIVE YOUR TRUTH
PRESS

DEDICATED TO THE
NATURAL SELF
IN ALL OF US

OTHER BOOKS BY CAROL TUTTLE

The Path to Wholeness

Remembering Wholeness

Dressing Your Truth—
Discover Your Type of Beauty

The Child Whisperer—
The Ultimate Handbook for Raising Happy,
Successful, and Cooperative Children

ACKNOWLEDGEMENTS

I WOULD LIKE TO thank the many people who have helped me better understand Energy Profiling^{SM} and how to teach it in a way that is simple and easily understood, resulting in quickly improving the quality of the lives of others.

Thank you to my family for living their true natures. My home has been a laboratory where I have discovered each Energy Type™, and it has provided me the perfect setting to observe and learn about the nature of each type.

My husband Jonathan expresses TYPE 2^{SM} Energy. Having this information in our marriage has been a godsend. Knowing each other's Energy Type has allowed us to respect the true nature of each other and support the full expression of it, eliminating the massive amount of frustration and effort that is too often spent trying to change one another.

Thank you to my oldest daughter Jenny and her husband Tony and our awesome grandsons, Seth, Joseph, and Neal. My grandchildren have shown me how early we begin to express our natural movement and tendencies of who we are.

I am grateful to my son Chris and his wife Sarah; my daughter Anne, her husband Tanner and their daughter Katie Claire; my son Mark and his wife Jaleah; and my son Mario.

As a mother, knowing the Energy Type of my family members has greatly assisted me in understanding and supporting the vast differences in how everyone in our family approaches every aspect of life, and how to support them in very different ways.

Thank you to Mike Fitzgerald, my editor. And to Kathy West for her editing assistance and understanding of this life-changing system. Both editors helped me create an easy-to-understand book with principles and information that is changing the lives of thousands.

And finally, thank you to the thousands of people who have gone through our Energy Profiling course over the last several years. Each of you has provided me with another insight to each Energy Type and how we are compelled to live it, even when we don't know it!

TABLE OF CONTENTS

INTRODUCTION

YOU TELL PEOPLE WHO you are by the way you walk into a room. They may not realize or know how to explain it, but others can sense the truth about you before you ever say a word. And what *is* the truth about you?

The truth is, at your very core, you express a unique, natural energy that influences how you approach new experiences, relate to people, manage challenges, and move through life in general. The truth is, your life runs better in every way when you understand your inner nature and live true to it, rather than fight against it.

Imagine experiencing more ease and happiness in your important relationships. Imagine being better heard and appreciated in your professional and social circles. Imagine living free of self-doubt and feeling clearer about your life's purpose. Imagine walking into any room or situation completely confident in your natural gifts and ability to understand others.

To those ends and more, I created an easy-to-understand model that I call the Energy Profiling system (2005). It is a human assessment tool to help you better understand your true, human nature. This tool has helped tens of thousands to create lives of greater balance, self-awareness, and inner confidence. It can support you in doing that, too.

People have been looking to understand themselves for a long time. For thousands of years, humans have been on a quest to better understand themselves and to better understand our human nature.

Personality profile systems have been around since 590 BC. The earliest recorded assessment tool is Ezekiel's Four Living Creatures in the Old Testament (Ezekiel 1:1–28). Other well-known profiling systems include Hippocrates' Four Humors (400 BC), Plato's Four Characters (340 BC), Aristotle's Four Sources of Happiness (325 BC), Galen's Four Temperaments (190) and, in modern times, Carl Jung's Psychological Types (1923), the Meyers-Briggs Type Indicator (1958), Hartman's Color Code (1987), and Keirsey's Four Temperaments (1998).

Even though describing people's general tendencies is obviously not a new idea, my approach to it is. The Energy Profiling system has the advantage of simpler, everyday, practical application, as this book will teach you. (I'm all about results!) This is also a more intuitive system, which means that the information you learn will free you up to be your best self, rather than box you into a category with a test.

For example, like many people, I took the Myers-Briggs Type Indicator® test in college. I also took the Color Code test and dabbled with the more ancient systems as a way to know myself better. I never found much practical use from these systems. I found the Myers-Briggs™ so complicated and detailed that I quickly lost interest. And I had no idea how to translate ENFP into practical use so that I could improve the quality of my life.

The Color Code test seemed to be based so strongly on personality that I questioned its accuracy, since so much of our personality can be tainted by our childhood environment. Because of the influence of our parents and families, answering a series of questions about our personality and behavior has limits and does not always give us an accurate reading of ourselves. Over time, we have all adapted to playing roles in an effort to get our emotional needs met, overriding our true natures in varying degrees as we play out these roles. I have seen this with hundreds of people in my career as an energy therapist. Personality and behavior alone seemed a weak barometer.

I was also hesitant to answer some of the questions honestly on personality assessments when it came to what I deemed "negative traits" about my personality. Who wants to admit to being overreactive and intense?

After taking these personality tests, the results told me which one of the four (or in the case of Myers Briggs, it was 16) groups I fell into. I did not like being reduced to one category and, ultimately, I did not like being told who I am. Through various approaches to teaching the Energy Profiling system, I have discovered that even though we think we want to be told who we are, no one really does!

With my strong opinion about personality profiling tests, why would I create another one? I certainly was not looking to create another profiling system on my career path, but here it is. In all honesty, the information catalyst to developing this Energy Profiling system found me and would not leave me alone! I believe the intelligence we call nature was trying to get through to me.

That's where this book begins. Together, we'll take a look at the world of nature and the four distinct expressions that show up there. We'll then look at how those expressions show up in every person, including you.

You'll then learn in depth about each of the four Energy Types and consider which one best describes your own dominant expression. At that point in the book, you might want to ask me the question that many people do: "What is my Energy Type?" My reply is always the same: "It is not my place to tell you who you are. Though you might think you want me to, what you really want is to discover that truth for yourself and then have it validated."

This is exactly what we wanted to experience as children— support for learning our true nature as we grew and developed, and feedback from our parents that validated this intrinsic truth through our growing years. Since that did not happen for many people, we act very childlike in our approach, looking to an authority of some kind to tell us who we are. As adults, we have referred to personality profiling and assessment tools for thousands of years as a resource to gather clues about ourselves and we have had the personality test tell us who we are. Then we resent and question what they say because we really don't like being told who we are!

I believe you know with a deep, inner confidence who you are. That is why this book will give you a framework and then teach you how to intuitively discover your own Energy Type (you won't find a questionnaire or a personality quiz in the back of this book).

After you've considered your own Energy Type, we'll take a look at how the four Energy Types impact your important relationships, your career, your fitness goals—and even how you get dressed every morning. We'll also have fun looking at where the four Energy Types show up in Hollywood and in politics. At the end of the book, you'll find additional resources to support you in your journey to live true to your nature.

I have come to love the Energy Profiling system. I love how simple it is, and how it has helped me understand myself and others more clearly. It has helped me respect others and forego old judgments I once had. With these tools in hand, I can see the nature of a person just by looking at them and gain rapport quickly. It has added value and improved the quality of my life in my role as a wife, mother, daughter, sister, and friend.

My hope is that this Energy Profiling system will be just that for you—a tool and resource to help you improve the quality of every area of your life.

I believe it is our God-given nature to remember our truth and then gain the confidence to live and express who we naturally are. As a teacher of spiritual principles and as a writer who has written in detail of the human experience of awakening to our true divine nature, I often hear the question, "Do you think our spirit's or soul's nature expresses itself in one of the Energy Types?" In other words, the question might be, "Would my spirit express a dominant TYPE 3^{SM} Energy?" I would say "No" to this question for a couple reasons.

First, I believe my soul is boundless and infinite beyond the expression we may perceive in this life. I believe I came into the physical world to take on a physical, human experience. In order for my soul to have that human experience, there needed to be a form that enabled me to experience human nature. I believe that form is experienced within the physical world as the expressions of movement I call Energy Types. Secondly, as I come to know my true human nature by knowing my Energy Type, I am more able to align with my true soul nature, which is infinite and expansive.

The Energy Profiling model is simple. Keep it that way for yourself. Don't overcomplicate it. Allow yourself to feel, see, and experience yourself and others in this simple and natural model that is easy to relate to and practical to apply in your everyday life.

God bless you to know your truth and live it with more fullness of heart.

—*Carol Tuttle*

It's Just My Nature!

A Guide to Knowing and Living Your True Nature

PART

- Our Connection with Nature
- Understanding the Energy Profiling System
- Get Profiled!

OUR CONNECTION WITH NATURE

WHEN YOU SAY THE WORD NATURE, what comes to your mind? Every time I have asked this question at an Energy Profiling class, I consistently hear the same responses: trees, the outdoors, wildlife, parks, forests, wilderness, animals, and so on. The response always references the expression of nature in the environment and wildlife of this planet.

Yet, we consistently use the word *nature* for another reference that we have paid little attention to—our human nature.

Have you ever heard yourself say, "It's just my nature"? Or how often have you referred to someone else, making comments like, "She's a natural at that," or "It's not their nature to be that way," or "They have so many natural gifts and talents"?

Have you ever wondered what you are referring to when you use the word *nature* when talking about people? I never did. I find it fascinating how much and how often we use the words *nature* and *natural* when referring to ourselves and other people. Not very often do we stop to think about what we are talking about and what we mean when we use these words.

How about "I am in my element!" or "They are in their element!" Have you thought about why we use the word *element*? You will.

As you read this book, you will see how the elements that make up wildlife and the outdoors are also deeply connected to you personally—influencing your body language, your physical structure, and even your personality more than you ever imagined.

Everything on this planet is created from the same four basic elements. These elements form the compounds and influence the dynamics of other elements, forming the building blocks of everything and everyone. These four elements are nitrogen, oxygen, hydrogen, and carbon.

In the metaphysical world, they are referred to as air, water, fire, and earth. The same movements expressed in the four elements are also found in the four states of matter: gas, liquid, plasma, and solid. Each of these four elements individually has a distinct energetic expression or movement. I call it the vibration and movement of the four Types of energy. They work together to form a whole. You very rarely find one element without the other. God used these four elements to create this planet, and all human beings were created to experience and enjoy it.

The same four elements that are expressed through mountains, trees, birds, rivers, lakes, animals, and rocks are expressed through each of us.

WHAT ALL THIS MEANS FOR YOU

You have the four basic elements within you in varying degrees. The combination of vibration and quality of each of these elements makes up your unique Energy Type—a description of the way you naturally move through every part of life.

Knowing your Energy Type empowers you to live a life of balance, self-awareness, and greater inner confidence. It gives you the why behind everything you do so that you can move through life in harmony with your true nature, rather than fight against it.

The difference between humans and the natural world is that nature, when not interfered with, maintains perfect balance. The intelligence in nature is a perfect system of balance; however, we humans have a great capacity to create imbalance.

As humans, we have the same potential to live in a natural state of balance within ourselves and each other. (There's that word *nature* again!) The difference between us and the rest of the natural world is our vast, thinking mind that creates opinions, conditions, values, and judgments in reference to who we are, how we act, what we say, what we do and basically how we live our lives. We have created a lot of false right and wrong against which we measure ourselves.

Whether or not you like or accept your Energy Type will depend on how much judgment you have created in respect to the movement of your core, true self.

For example, I tell my students that a willow tree is content just being a willow tree—a movement of fluid and flowing expression. It does not have a conscious mind to consider that it would rather be a quaking aspen because the quaking aspen appears to have more fun—expressing itself more randomly, flickering and popping in the wind.

We do not necessarily see ourselves as vibration and movement. Yet that is how we see and experience nature all around us.

People travel thousands of miles to see and experience beautiful expressions of the natural world. What we experience is the movement of nature speaking to us. Years ago, we noticed we had the capacity to interfere with the natural world in obliterating species of animals and environments, so we created laws to protect the animals and secure the lands so we could continue to enjoy the expressions they offer us. We need to appreciate and personally protect our true selves' natural expressions, as well.

How many times have you visited a beautiful place or seen wildlife in a natural environment? When you visit these places in nature, do you look at the scenery and judge it to be unacceptable? For example, if you have visited or are familiar with the Grand Canyon, you will know that the landscape there is very rugged, rough, textured, dry, dynamic, substantial, and very rich in color. It is a spectacular expression of the natural world. Would you judge it to be ugly, old, too much intensity, or unacceptable to you? Not at all. You experience the scenery and movement of this grand place and love it. Yet do you experience your own appearance or personality as spectacular expressions of who you are? Or do you judge them to be unacceptable and inferior as you compare yourself to someone else who expresses themselves differently than you do?

When you learn your Energy Type, I hope you will open your heart as wide to yourself as you do to the natural world. I hope you will take all your self-imposed judgments that you have created, deem them to be no longer acceptable, and throw them away.

You have been created to express your natural gifts and talents in a balanced and beautiful way, just as the natural world has. Knowing your natural gifts and talents better through knowing your Energy Type will support you in living a life of balance. The degree to which you accept or judge your natural gifts, talents, and tendencies will be determined by what you believe is acceptable or unacceptable in your own movement and expression.

You have perceived yourself largely through the eyes of collective feedback—what others have told you or how they have responded to you. Early in our lives, we fool ourselves and believe the power and authority to assess ourselves is outside of us, in the form of parents and other authority figures. As adults, we continue to live this lie by continuing to believe what we were told, and by imposing our judgments on our children and others.

IT IS TIME

It is time for you to reclaim your power. Choose to live as the power source and creator of your life. It is time to see your true self, your natural self. Embrace your vibration and movement. Find yourself. Peel away the layers of judgment and illusion of who you are not, to discover who you are. Knowing your Energy Type will make all the difference in knowing and loving who you are.

You are a part of the whole expression of nature. Learn from the birds, trees, rivers, animals, mountains, and rocks to be who you are and love it.

There is a reason for your natural gifts and tendencies in the expression of you. There is a purpose that brings us together as humanity to live in harmony and balance with each other and with nature.

As you read this book, allow yourself to feel whatever comes up for you. The true power of who you are has been locked away in the pockets of your hidden emotion of shame and the illusion that you are inadequate. Use this book to validate your truth and the truth of others.

Use the Energy Profiling model as a tool to support you rather than a system to define you.

Have fun with this as you claim the truth and live who you truly are!

Understanding the Energy Profiling System

ENERGY PROFILING IS A human assessment tool. Looking at the four elements that create all of nature—nitrogen/air, oxygen/water, hydrogen/fire, and carbon/earth—we consider the vibration and movement of each element and how these innate movements express through people.

You are created from all four of these elements. As an individual, you express your own unique composition of all four elements. You express the movement of one of the four elements more dominantly than you do any of the other three. This is your dominant Energy Type and tells the most about your natural tendencies.

ENERGY PROFILING BASICS

For simplicity in the model of Energy Profiling, we refer to each of the elements expressing in people as TYPE 1^{SM} Energy, TYPE 2^{SM} Energy, TYPE 3^{SM} Energy, and TYPE 4^{SM} Energy.

The Energy Profiling methodology is empirically based, meaning the principles of the Energy Profiling system can be consistently observed through all of nature, including human beings.

The Energy Profiling system helps you better understand your core true self by using movement as the primary measurement of assessment. The Energy Profiling model looks deeper than personality and behavior. We can assess how the vibration and movement of each of the elements expresses through all of nature and each of us.

"I think the single most helpful thing that I learned from the profiling class was to look at my oldest son whose energy and personality is completely opposite from mine in a new light. I realized that some of his dominant energy traits, which I had perceived as weaknesses, were his strengths, and that I had been trying to make him be more like me. It was helpful on my path to building up and not breaking down what has become a very loving and peaceful relationship between us. Also, it was a wonderfully helpful thing to realize that life is so much more enjoyable when we can allow each other to be what God intended us to be and then grow from there."
—STACIE LINDSEY (TYPE 4ˢᴹ ENERGY), UTAH

Your dominant Energy Type is the most prevailing expression influencing all aspects of your life and it never changes over time. Even when you try to override it and change your personality, this core movement cannot be silenced. You see it expressing most innately when you are not thinking about it. It expresses in ways that we don't judge readily, like walking, talking, doodling, and laughing, just to name a few examples. It is when we are not consciously thinking about who we are, that our true nature expresses itself most naturally.

There are four Types of energy that together, create your whole profile. I believe we are each unique in the creation and expression of who we are, yet I have found an uncanny similarity in the tendencies of expression found in people of the same dominant Energy Type. We are each unique and also very much the same within our Energy Type.

BENEFITS OF KNOWING YOUR ENERGY TYPE

The Energy Profiling model is a simple, yet profound tool that helps us clearly understand our natural gifts and talents, our strengths and weaknesses, our approach to life, our ways of processing and perceiving our life experience, and how we process information and make decisions. It helps us understand that we were created to express these core movements in every aspect of our lives, and to enjoy who we are created to be within our human experience.

When we live in conscious alignment with our dominant Energy Type and how all four Energy Types interact within us, we experience a balanced life. We have an expanded awareness in our perception and understanding of others. I have experienced many relationships coming into more harmony and rapport as a result of knowing my own Energy Type and the Energy Type of others.

I have received hundreds of testimonials from people who have personally benefited from this information. They have raved to me about how much their relationships with others improved. Clients have even commented to me that they feel their divorces could possibly have been avoided if they had had this knowledge and insight to help them understand each other better. I have had numerous parents share that this was the missing puzzle piece that completely explained why they got along better with certain children and had continuous struggles with another.

All the Energy Types stand equal in their value. There is not one more gifted or capable than another.

Everyone has the right and opportunity to be successful, ambitious, determined, fun, loving, caring, prosperous, generous, enlightened—all the qualities we seek in our human experience. What will look different is the way we move and express ourselves in our pursuit of these qualities.

"Your Energy Profiling class was life-changing for me. I was so excited to learn what Energy TYPE 1^{SM} was because instinctively I knew that I was not living in my true Energy Type. As each Energy Type was explained, I knew that I was living in TYPE

4^{SM} Energy but it was not until the slide show was presented and I looked in the mirror that I saw that I was an obvious TYPE 1^{SM} Energy.

"I dutifully stood by the TYPE 1^{SM} Energy picture because that is what I looked like. I then took the yellow sheet of paper and read through it and realized that is what I used to live until I got married 38 years ago. Over time I thought I had to be someone else to please my husband—it was not safe to be me. I now feel that I have been liberated!

"I know that this is my special gift, that there is nothing wrong with me. I have found my voice and I am expressing my feelings and emotions. How is my family reacting to this? My four adult daughters are taking it all in and saying, 'You go for it Mom— you look great and alive!' My husband is saying, 'You are not the person I married.' It is obvious to me it will take time for him to adjust to the real me. But there is no turning back—I am empowered by knowing and living my truth! Thank you again."

—RUTH CLAWSON (TYPE 1^{SM} ENERGY), UTAH

HOW CAN EVERY PERSON BE CATEGORIZED INTO JUST 4 TYPES?

At first glance, you might have wondered how I could possibly describe everyone—including you—using just four categories. After all, people everywhere are so unique. I understand and respect your response.

Consider for just a moment how many sophisticated things in our world are made from just a few simple building blocks. Color, for instance. All the colors in the world are made by mixing together only three primary colors: red, yellow, and blue. These primary colors are the foundation, not a limitation to the number of unique colors in our world.

Every person's natural movement is built from the energy of four basic elements, yet every one of us is unique. We do have many common tendencies and gifts due to sharing similar dominant Energy Types, but as you read, you'll find that this information is empowering and freeing, not limiting. With that in mind, let's talk about the science behind the 4 Energy Types.

My friend, Deborah Miller, who has studied my model of Energy Profiling in depth, has her Ph.D. in cell and molecular biology. She shared the following insight with me:

"How can you relate the quantities of these elements (nitrogen, oxygen, hydrogen and carbon), which have relatively fixed amounts in every human being, to the four Energy Types and how they are expressed in you? Let's take a look at this from a scientific perspective.

"At this time, scientific studies about the actual amounts of elements in each of the four Energy Types have not been done, but we can draw some conclusions about how small changes in element quantities could create the different natural movements in humans that are expressing through the natural tendencies of each Energy Type. For example, some people might think that if their element was oxygen (a TYPE 2^{SM} Energy), that would mean they have more of that element than the other Types. Technically, that could be true, but we are talking about miniscule differences in actual amounts, not just more oxygen. Since the quantity of each of these four elements in every human being is almost the same (*almost* is the key word here), a small change in the amount of these elements does make a difference. Why? Oxygen, nitrogen, hydrogen, and carbon are the elements that make up the four bases (adenine, guanine, cytosine, and thymine) which make up our DNA. Changes in the DNA structure, sometimes as small as a single position, can cause small or significant changes in the human body.

"Let me give you a couple of examples of small changes that make a difference to how the item or substance appears and the effects produced.

"Details on a shirt. We can all agree that a button-down shirt has a back, two front panels, sleeves and a collar. Let's say this shirt is white. What happens when you change the buttons on this shirt? The shirt is still a shirt. Plain, simple, white buttons would give the shirt a dressed down look whereas some sparkly bright red buttons would give it a lively, upbeat, dressed-up look. These details make a difference in the look or how the shirt expresses itself, but they don't make the shirt into a pair of pants.

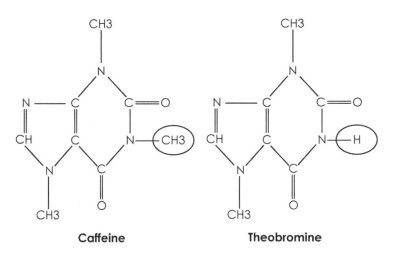

Caffeine   **Theobromine**

"Caffeine vs. Theobromine. I think most people would agree that the effect of coffee on the human body is different than that of chocolate. Why is that? Both have stimulants in them; coffee has caffeine and chocolate has theobromine. In fact, these stimulants have almost exactly the same structure. They look identical—except for a change in one position. See the circled part in the images of the two molecules.

"That change in one position (a carbon with three hydrogens in caffeine instead of one hydrogen in theobromine) causes a big difference in their effects. For example, coffee's caffeine is intense, strong, fast-acting and even causes the jitters and mental stress, whereas chocolate's theobromine is gentle, mild, longer lasting, and is a mild antidepressant creating that "feel good" effect of chocolate. The amount of elements different in these molecules is minimal, but the difference in effect or expression is significant.

"Now you can see how apparently small changes can make a difference in effect or expression. Let's go back to humans and the quantities of elements and their expression. For example, all human DNA is 99.9 percent the same. Yes, your DNA is 99.9 percent the same as all other human beings. Only 0.1 percent is different. That means the diversity in humans comes from that 0.1 percent that is different (I'm not including learned behaviors or socialization). For example, this 0.1 percent accounts for sizes (tall to short), shapes (thin to robust), colors (all skin tones), sometimes health (genetic diseases, for example) and more. The overall quantity of each of these four elements in each human being is relatively the same, yet with small differences in particular positions, the outcome can be very different.

"Remember you are a unique combination of these four elements; therefore, you have a unique expression. As a scientist, I see this uniqueness as the following: the quantity of each element, their positions and how they are expressed are seen in your innate movement and vibration, which create your Energy Type as described within the model of Energy Profiling. With a conscious understanding of your Energy Type, you are able to more effectively express who you actually are."

At its core, the model of Energy Profiling is an assessment tool based on movement. Movement applies to every person on the planet, transcending race, culture, ethnic background, and personality. Once you discover your Energy Type and better understand the nature of your own core movement, you will open yourself up to new possibilities and greater confidence. Time to get started.

Get Profiled!

DISCOVERING YOUR ENERGY TYPE is an intuitive, personal process. I will not offer you a personality questionnaire, nor give you any other resource that tells you who you are. You read the material about each of the 4 Energy Types in the upcoming chapters, and then you identify which of the Types resonates with you most. It's as simple as that.

As you read about each of the Energy Types, open yourself up to who you really are. Pay attention to your heart more than your head. Your mind will tell you who you think you are but your heart just knows it.

As you walk through the Energy Profiling process, you will see yourself in each Energy Type—how the vibration and movement of each Energy Type influences your personality traits, behavior tendencies, brain and thought processes, gifts and talents, personal space, body language, and physical features. You have all four elements of nitrogen/air, oxygen/water, hydrogen/fire, and carbon/ earth inherently in you to varying degrees.

Everyone has a dominant Energy Type that does not change in his or her lifetime. When assessing yourself, look and feel which of the four Energy Types most typifies you.

WHY NO QUESTIONNAIRE?

When the Energy Profiling system first came into being, we used to end each live class with a questionnaire much like the ones already out there in other profiling systems. You could choose from four possibilities, add up your score, and then look to your test results to tell you which Energy Type you were.

But a higher percentage of error results when we just look at personality and behavior (especially when only using a questionnaire). I believe you innately know who you are and, as you consider the information about each of the Energy Types, you will know which one resonates with you most. As you validate your inner nature, you take on a new level of ownership and permission to be yourself.

We also have a safeguard for error that allows us to see more clearly what your core nature is. This is the part of the Energy Profiling system we call Body Profiling™.

In Body Profiling, we can assess how the movement of each Energy Type expresses through your physical features. This allows us a default mechanism to look beyond personality and get a more accurate reading of who you truly are.

For example, I can easily determine someone's dominant Energy Type by simple assessments and movements in their body—that is, how they walk into a room, their demeanor when coming into a room of people they do not know, how they behave during a class, how they move through the process of learning new material, and the types of questions they ask, if they ask any.

You will be introduced to the basics of profiling this way in our resources. You will learn to look at your physical features in a new way. You likely have never looked at your nose and wondered if it holds clues about your personality. With Body Profiling, you will look at your cheeks, eyebrows, and smile in a whole new light!

As I mentioned before, we used to offer an assessment test at the end of our trainings. One night at the end of an Energy Profiling class, I watched the most amazing thing happen. Our Energy Profiling classes were three hours long. The first two-and-a-half hours of the class, we taught through lecture, story, symbol, visuals and question-and-answer sessions. After this first part of the class, we handed out the traditional question and answer profiling tests, having the participants choose one of four responses from a series of multiple questions to determine their Energy Type. I saw the participants go from an intuitive connection of sensing who they were to a logical assessment, referring to their test results as the primary feedback to tell them who they were.

We decided to experiment in our next class and eliminate the end-of-class assessment test—rather, we asked the participants to look within themselves and follow their heart and choose which Energy Type they were dominant in.

In the training center where we held our first classes—The Center for Living Your Truth in Draper, Utah—we displayed four images of art on the walls that depicted the movement and expression of each Energy Type. At the end of the class, we asked the participants to go stand by which image they felt depicted their dominant Energy Type. We then had our Experts roam around the room, interacting with each participant, assessing their Body Profile and validating whether they were in the right place based on what we saw in the body. By the end of the night, we felt confident everyone has been assessed accurately. We ultimately told the participants to follow their own hearts and that it was not our place to tell them who they were. We were honest about what we saw in their body to give them feedback since we are experts in the Body Profiling process, but we allowed each participant to decide their dominant Energy Type.

Marcy (TYPE 1^{SM} Energy) shared this story about her neighbor, who Marcy invited to come to an Energy Profiling class with her. Marcy had already had a marvelous experience learning her profile and seeing where in her life where she was not honoring her true nature.

She had attended the Dressing Your Truth Ultimate Makeover Event at Red Mountain Spa, which took her experience to another level. She was so thrilled by how much this program had improved the quality of her life that she wanted her friend to experience this for herself. Her friend attended a class and when it came time for her to pick her Energy Type, she went and stood in the TYPE 2^{SM} Energy section.

As I do when I am teaching the class, I roamed around the room and shared feedback with anyone who did not appear to be in their right Energy Type according to what I saw in their Body Profile. When I came to Marcy's friend, I asked her, "What would be your next choice for your Energy Type if this is not right for you?" She hesitated and replied, "Maybe TYPE 1^{SM} Energy." I told her, "That is what I am seeing in your face." I invited her to go stand in the TYPE 1^{SM} section and see how that felt. She agreed and I noticed that she came back to the TYPE 2^{SM} Energy section after a little time had passed. As I did in those classes, I offered the feedback based on Body Profile assessment, and then allowed clients to know for themselves.

Marcy's friend left that night trying to convince herself she expressed dominant TYPE 2^{SM} Energy. Marcy shared the rest of the story with me just recently. Her friend went home and that night had the worst night's sleep ever. She called Marcy and shared how confused she was. The next night, she was restless again and, finally fed up and frustrated, took off her TYPE 2^{SM} watch, threw it across the room and yelled, "I am not a 2. I am a 1!"

The Energy Profiling system's information spoke to her on a deep innate level that she could not deny. She wrestled with it in her mind, and discovered that she had been unnecessarily wrestling with her identity for many years. She is now happily living true to her nature, and living life with more zest and bounce, which is totally her!

Discovering your Energy Type is truly is more of a right brain, intuitive personal experience. When we operate more from heart than logic, we have a much better sense of who we are. When logic is our reference to who we are, we often get confused, conflicted, and question our innate nature.

To help you know and live your true nature, I have created three assessment tools and made them available to help you assess yourself, particularly your dominant Energy Type.

The resources I have created to support you are:

1. This book
2. Our online interactive, multi-media Energy Profiling assessment resources at www.myenergyprofile.com
3. The Carol Blog. On The Carol Blog, you will find frequent posts about the Energy Profiling system, with real-life examples and practical tips on living true to your nature. I share more about each of the four Energy Types and how the energy of each Type expresses in real people. The Carol Blog is a fun and entertaining way to continue your study and increase your knowledge of each Type. www.thecarolblog.com

The book, the Energy Profiling website, and The Carol Blog support each other beautifully and will support you in learning more and becoming more aware of your own Energy Type.

This book provides information about each Energy Type in depth. You can review it as often as you would like and gain more insight from studying each Energy Type.

Since we have just a few visuals in this book, I encourage you to experience our online Energy Profiling assessment experience at www.myenergyprofile.com. This website offers you a free interactive course with many visuals and videos that are not available in this book. Here you will see what I mean when I teach concepts like circle cheeks, a chiseled chin, a triangular nose, or pictures of nature that show a constant, still movement compared to a light, upward movement. The visuals on the website support you with a visual experience, which is extremely helpful in relating to the movements of each Energy Type and understanding your own true nature.

It is my goal to continue to provide you, as an Energy Profiling student, with practical and useful information that gives you the opportunity to make this system useful in every aspect of your life. As you will learn, Body Profiling is one of the most telling standards of assessment in determining your dominant Energy Type. The Carol Blog features video posts where you can learn more about Body Profiling and how to use it in determining your Energy Type.

PART

- AN OVERVIEW OF THE FOUR ENERGY TYPES
- THE FOUR ENERGY TYPES IN NATURE
- THE FOUR ENERGY TYPES IN PEOPLE

An Overview of the Four Energy Types

THE FOUR ENERGY TYPES reflect the movement of the four elements that create everything in this world, the natural world, and humans. Here is a general overview of each Energy Type. This overview shows the element, natural expression and movement that each one reflects.

THE FOUR ENERGY TYPES AND THE ELEMENTS THEY DEPICT

- TYPE 1^{SM} Energy—Nitrogen/air
- TYPE 2^{SM} Energy—Oxygen/water
- TYPE 3^{SM} Energy—Hydrogen/fire
- TYPE 4^{SM} Energy—Carbon/earth

THE PRIMARY VIBRATION AND MOVEMENT DISTINCTIVE TO EACH ENERGY TYPE

- TYPE 1^{SM} Energy—Upward, light movement
- TYPE 2^{SM} Energy—Fluid, flowing movement
- TYPE 3^{SM} Energy—Active, reactive movement
- TYPE 4^{SM} Energy—Constant, still movement

DESCRIPTIVE WORDS CHARACTERISTIC
OF EACH ENERGY TYPE

- TYPE 1^{SM} Energy: Upward, light, random, disconnected, buoyant, free, crisp, fresh, bright, unstructured, spontaneous, brilliant, and upbeat

- TYPE 2^{SM} Energy: Fluid, flowing, soft, connected, easy, relaxed, subtle, blended, inviting, comfortable, steady, and muted

- TYPE 3^{SM} Energy: Active, reactive, angular, substantial, sure, textured, rich, dynamic, swift, and irregular

- TYPE 4^{SM} Energy: Constant, still, bold, clean, simple, structured, regal, clear, precise, reflective, high contrast, and keen

THE DISTINCT MOVEMENTS AND SHAPES
OF EACH ENERGY TYPE

These movements express in both nature and people.

TYPE 1^{SM} Energy moves upward and out. It is a random movement that disconnects and connects readily and effortlessly:

TYPE 2^{SM} Energy moves in a steady downward flow. Cascading gently and easily, always staying connected on its course:

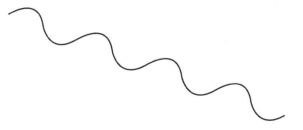

TYPE 3^{SM} Energy moves swiftly and dynamically in an irregular course. It is a confident, sure movement that always leaves an impression or evidence that the movement was there:

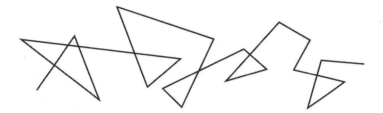

TYPE 4^{SM} Energy is a constant, steady movement that moves from one point to another with exactness, like a straight line. When there is no movement, or stillness, it creates a solid structure:

The vibration and movement of each Energy Type can also be depicted as different shapes.

TYPE 1^{SM} Energy: Circles, stars, spirals, curlicues, dots, hearts, all animated shapes:

TYPE 2^{SM} Energy: Elongated S, teardrop, oval, soft rectangle, any shape with a soft edge:

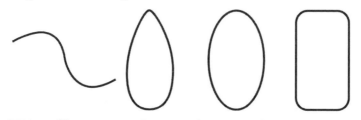

TYPE 3^{SM} Energy: Angles, triangles, rectangles, geometric shapes with right angles, any shape with a point:

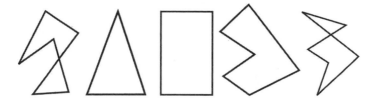

TYPE 4^{SM} Energy: Elongated oval with straight sides, elongated rectangle, fast parallel lines in any direction:

The following shows a simple graph comparing the movement of each Type on a scale that represents a low to high movement of the four Energy Types.

TYPE 1^{SM} Energy is the highest movement.
TYPE 2^{SM} Energy is medium to medium-low.
TYPE 3^{SM} Energy is medium to medium-high.
TYPE 4^{SM} Energy is low to no movement.

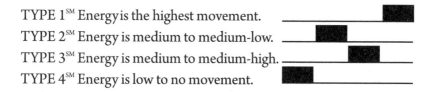

INTROVERSION AND EXTROVERSION IN EACH ENERGY TYPE

The natural movement of each Energy Type can be either an extrovert or introvert expression. What I mean by extrovert is the motion of the energy moving outward, away from its source. Introvert energy moves inward to its source or is still and reflective. The extrovert/introvert nature of each Energy Type is:

- TYPE 1ˢᴹ Energy: Extrovert energy, moving randomly outward away from its source

- TYPE 2ˢᴹ Energy: Introvert energy, moving subtly inward towards its source

- TYPE 3ˢᴹ Energy: Extrovert energy, moving dynamically outward away from its source

- TYPE 4ˢᴹ Energy: Introvert energy that is still and reflective

YIN YANG QUALITIES OF EACH ENERGY TYPE

The concept of Yin Yang, which comes to us from ancient Chinese philosophy, describes how seemingly opposing forces are interdependent in the natural world. Each Energy Type has its own Yin Yang quality.

The quality of yin energy is light, soft, still, and moving inward to create. The quality of yang energy is radiant, firm, dynamic, and moving outward to create.

Yin Yang energy always exists in partnership, offering complimentary expressions. There is a Yin Yang partnership to each Energy Type and to the entire Energy Profiling system as a whole. Each Energy Type expresses the essence of either yin or yang. To know the Yin Yang quality of each Energy Type, we consider whether the movement is soft or firm, and if the energy moves outward, inward, or is still.

The Yin Yang nature of each Energy Type is:

- **TYPE 1**^{SM} Energy: Yin/Yang. Yin for its fresh, light quality. Yang for its outward, radiant quality.

- **TYPE 2**^{SM} Energy: Yin/Yin. Yin for its soft, subtle quality. Yin for its inward, relaxed quality.

- **TYPE 3**^{SM} Energy: Yang/Yang. Yang for its dynamic, angular quality. Yang for its outward, intense quality.

- **TYPE 4**^{SM} Energy: Yang/Yin. Yang for its firm, bold quality. Yin for its still, reflective quality.

The Four Energy Types in Nature

THE FOUR ENERGY TYPES are expressed everywhere in the natural world. Nature is movement. Here are just a few examples of the 4 Energy Types expressing in the natural world.

TYPE 1ˢᴹ ENERGY

Imagine a scene in nature of rolling hills with beautiful meadows. Spontaneous flowers pop up in brilliant colors. A babbling brook runs through the vivacious meadow, and a bunny rabbit hops by.

TYPE 1ˢᴹ movement in nature expresses itself as upward, light, random, disconnected, buoyant, animated, crisp, fresh, bright, non-structured, spontaneous, brilliant, and upbeat. We feel this way when we are in natural settings that express this movement.

Examples of TYPE 1ˢᴹ Energy in nature include:

Tree: Quaking Aspen. Its leaves are circular, it has shallow roots, and grows in clusters or groves, does not do well growing by itself. Its leaves turn a brilliant shade of gold and are the first to turn color in the fall. Palm. It grows straight up and shoots up and out at the top. It bares circular-shaped fruit. We relate palm trees to vacation and having fun. Cherry. See the tree in blossom with sprays of pink or white.

Wildlife: Rabbits. Rabbits bounce, hop, and move buoyantly. They twitch their noses quickly. Dolphins. Dolphins are highly intelligent with acute senses. They are very social, living in pods.

31

Where food is abundant, smaller pods create super pods, adapting easily to larger groups. They have an altruistic nature, helping other dolphins when needed, even bringing them to the surface if they are injured and need air. Playing and jumping is an important part of a dolphin's life.

Water: Babbling Brook. A babbling brook moves randomly over rocks and stones, making a popping sound as it moves. Boiling water with steam rising. Boiling water pops and bubbles in a circle shape, turning into steam that moves upward and out. Old Faithful. Old Faithful is a cone geyser located in Yellowstone National Park in the U.S. state of Wyoming. It shoots water and vapor up and outward in a forceful spray called an eruption. The eruptions occur intermittently and are unpredictable.

Bird: Hummingbird. A hummingbird rapidly flaps its wings flying from flower to flower, gathering nectar. They can hover in mid-air and are the only birds that fly backwards.

Flower: Daisy, Sunflower, Tulip. Each of these flowers expresses a sunny, fresh, light, happy mood.

Dog: Chihuahua. Chihuahuas are prized for their devotion, ferocity, and personality. They are easily adaptable to a variety of environments. Very quick to learn commands, they are easily trained to perform tricks. Chihuahuas also tend to have a clannish nature, often preferring the companionship of other Chihuahuas over other dogs.

Sun/Moon Cycles: Sunrise. The rising of the sun represents a new day, a new beginning, and a fresh start on life. The sun is bright, cheery, and uplifting in the morning.

Insect: Butterfly. Butterflies have brightly colored wings with random, animated patterns. They have erratic, buoyant flight patterns.

State of Matter: Gas. In a gas, the molecules have a high energy, are far apart from each other, and can move around quickly. A gas has no definite shape or volume, but occupies the entire container in which it is confined.

TYPE 2^{SM} ENERGY

Imagine a scene in nature of a large and languid river like the great Mississippi. Slow and steady water forms a deep and steady path. The banks of the river are lined with tall and sweeping willow trees. You come to sit by the river, relaxing under the tree as you contemplate life, where you have come from and where you are going, much like the river at your feet.

TYPE 2^{SM} movement in nature expresses itself as fluid, flowing, soft, connected, easy, relaxed, subtle, blended, elegant, comfortable, steady, muted.

Examples of TYPE 2^{SM} Energy in nature include:

Tree: Weeping Willow. The leaves are an elongated S curve and the roots grow very deep. The long branches move gently, subtly in a breeze.

Wildlife: Elephant. Elephants are large and muscular with all rounded edges on their body. They are thick skinned and stick together in social groups. They are a symbol of wisdom in Asian cultures.

Water: Mississippi River. The Mississippi is the largest river system in the United States. It moves deep and steady. Water flowing and cascading from a tipped-over glass. The water never separates. It always flows in a steady stream.

Bird: Dove. Doves are soft and blended in texture and coloring. The dove is a symbol of peace and comfort.

Flower: Rose. A rose has soft, oval-shaped petals. It is often a symbol of love and connecting at the heart.

Dog: Afghan Hound. These dogs move gracefully and have a long, flowing coat, with a long S curve to their body shape.

Sun/Moon Cycles: Dusk. After the sun has set and before it grows dark, we slow down, come to the end of our daylight and feel the need to relax. At dusk the sky is very soft and blended, and the lighting is subtle and muted.

Insect: Caterpillar. A caterpillar is soft and moves in an S curve. It takes on the coloring of the plant species it lives on so it will blend into the background.

State of Matter: Liquid. When a solid is heated above its melting point, it becomes liquid. Liquids adapt and conform to the shape of their container. The molecules of liquids also tend to stay together in one mass.

TYPE 3ˢᴹ ENERGY

Imagine a scene in nature like the Grand Canyon. There you find rustic, angular shapes with substantial, textured plateaus. The colors are rich and earthy. There is a sense of awe for the power that has moved the earth to create this dynamic setting.

TYPE 3ˢᴹ movement in nature expresses itself as active, reactive, angular, substantial, sure, textured, rich, dynamic, swift, and irregular. The initial action creates a reaction or a result.

Examples of TYPE 3ˢᴹ Energy in nature include:

Tree: Maple Tree. The maple tree grows in the shape of a triangle. Its leaves are angular and turn the color of rich shades

in the fall. Its trunk is very textured, and many varieties are grown to produce maple syrup.

Wildlife: Tiger and Lion. Tigers and lions are very powerful, swift animals. They have beautiful, rich-colored coats and heavily textured manes. They have powerfully built legs and shoulders, with the result that they have the ability to pull down prey substantially heavier than themselves.

Water: Water coming forcefully out of a faucet, filling a tub. The purpose of the water flow is to fill the tub so you can take a bath quickly, an action that creates a result. Niagara Falls. Niagara Falls are massive waterfalls on the Niagara River, straddling the international border, separating the Canadian Province of Ontario and the U.S. state of New York. The enormous energy of Niagara Falls has long been utilized as an enormous source of power, harnessing the power to create electricity.

Bird: Hawk. This bird is very rich in color, has angular wings, and swiftly dives after its prey.

Flower: Tiger Lily. This flower is angular and textured and very substantial in size.

Dog: German Shepherd. German Shepherds are swift to learn commands and are large and aggressive dogs. German Shepherds are a very popular selection for use as working dogs and law enforcement.

Sun/Moon Cycles: Sunsets. As the sun is setting, the sky grows rich in dramatic color. The light forms angular shapes and the horizon appears to be very textured.

Insect: Cockroach, Bee, Ant. Cockroaches are amongst the hardiest of insects on the planet. They are very thick-skinned and resourceful insects. Bees and ants are both determined, working towards an end result.

State of Matter: Plasma. 99 percent of the universe is made of plasma. The Earth is surrounded by it. The aurora borealis is a lovely example of it. So is lightning. The sun is made of it. Plasma has magnetic and electric fields that move around rambunctiously and unpredictably, altering their environment. As the environment changes, so does the plasma—a continuous dance of action and reaction. Sounds like me cleaning my kitchen! (I'm a TYPE 3^{SM}.)

TYPE 4^{SM} ENERGY

Imagine a scene in nature of a majestic, snow-capped mountain next to a large, still, reflective mountain lake. The exact image of the mountain is being mirrored in the lake. Or see the image of a solid iceberg standing motionless in a vast ocean. Or imagine newly fallen snow, clean and smooth. All these images leave you breathless and respectful of the strong, bold expressions of nature.

TYPE 4^{SM} movement in nature expresses itself as constant, still, bold, clean, simple, structured, regal, clear, precise, reflective, keen and with high contrast.

Examples of TYPE 4^{SM} Energy in nature include:

Tree: Noble Fir. These trees grow tall and erect. Their branches come out of the trunk evenly, and needles grow parallel to the ground. Even in the wind they are very still and motionless due to their rigid structure. When cut, they remain green and vital longer than other coniferous trees.

Wildlife: Black Panther, Panda Bear, Polar Bear, Penguin. Each of these animals exhibits a regal nature and appearance.

They have sleek lines and saturated coats. The high contrast of black and white reflect simple, clean lines. Penguins, for example, are very loyal to their young, going to great lengths and sacrifice to keep them alive in very severe conditions.

Water: Icicles, a frozen ice cube, and a still pond. Each exhibits a quality of structure and stillness.

Bird: Swan. The regal swan exhibits style and elegance. They mate for life and are very clean birds. The rare black swan stands out in bold contrast to its white counterpart.

Flower: Calla Lily. This flower is so refined it has the appearance of being sculpted. Long-stemmed rosebud. A single, long-stemmed rosebud is a beautiful and simple expression of love and loyalty.

Dog: Alaskan Husky. Alaskan Huskies are highly efficient sled dogs that are known for their incredible endurance in racing long distances, being able to stay focused getting from point A to point B!

Sun/Moon Cycles: Full Moon. The full moon reflecting against a dark night sky creates a high contrast and makes a bold statement.

Insect: Spider. Spiders live alone. They build symmetrical webs that require great care and focus. They wait in a very still manner for their prey.

State of Matter: Solid. The particles (ions, atoms or molecules) are packed closely together. The forces between particles are strong enough that the particles do not move as freely as in other states. As a result, a solid has a stable, definite shape.

The Energy Profiling system gives you a new lens to see the world. You may find yourself starting to profile a lot of different things in this world! For example, when I took a trip to Thailand, I had the opportunity to experience the wildlife of that beautiful land. All in one day, my group and I visited an elephant training camp, a tiger reserve, and a monkey show. Being so close to the animals, we really had a chance to experience their natural movement—their Energy Type.

While riding an elephant (TYPE 2^{SM} Energy), I noticed the strong and steady movement of the elephant. Each step up a muddy slope was methodical. The elephant took his time to make sure his next step would be steady. He moved deliberately with care.

We visited a tiger (TYPE 3^{SM} Energy) reserve where we were able to go into the tiger habitat. We were given careful instructions on how to move around the tigers so as to not cause them to pounce or swipe at us with their swift and powerful paws.

Our last stop was to see a monkey (TYPE 1^{SM} Energy) show. Several monkeys had been trained to do tricks and entertain the audience with their animated antics and friendly interaction. Experiencing the expressions of each of these Energy Types enriched my own life.

Nature is filled with all four movements of the four Energy Types. Have some fun paying more attention to this movement, and how it enhances your mood and spirit.

The Four Energy Types in People

NOW THIS IS WHERE the Energy Profiling system really gets fun! It is uncanny how consistently the movement of the four Energy Types expresses through people. I respect the fact that we are all created to be our own unique, expressive selves. But after you read the next few sections, I think you will agree that all of us express remarkable similarities in certain key ways that can be described in four group. Sure, within these groups you will find unique differences, but the general tendencies you will come to notice in aspects of our human expression are certainly there.

I have consistently found that the vibration and movement of each of the four Energy Types expresses through many aspects of our human experience. In the following sections, we will look at where and how the vibration and movement of each Energy Type is expressed in the following aspects of our human nature.

Gifts and Talents: The natural movement of our dominant Energy Type supports us in having a unique gift and talent that not only adds great value to our own life, but contributes to the wholeness of humanity working in harmony. What is ironic is that quite often we judge the very gift nature endowed us with to be a weakness and a flaw. Knowing your natural gifts and talents that are supported by your dominant Energy Type will be amazingly supportive and freeing to you.

Personality Traits: Even though we can consciously manipulate our personality to play roles and hide our true nature in these roles, we still see the expressions of each Energy Type pushing through all of these roles, insisting on being expressed naturally. These natural expressions cannot be silenced, but they can be restrained, shamed, judged, and deemed unacceptable. Most likely what you have disliked about yourself or judged unacceptable could be your natural self and who you truly are. This is one of the most important concepts of the Energy Profiling system.

Thought and Feeling Processes: The four Energy Types are the most expressive in our inner world of thoughts and feelings. The inner world creates the outer world. It all begins with our inner thoughts and feelings. This is our own personal space that we can never step outside of. You are always experiencing you.

Everything in your outer world is a reflection of your inner world. How you perceive your reality is being influenced by your dominant Energy Type. Your dominant Energy Type is influencing what you value in yourself and others.

Behavior Tendencies: These include how we express the natural movement of the four Energy Types in our communication, personal relationships, social interaction, work, physical activity, and management of money.

Body Language: It could all come down to how you doodle! Doodling is one of the most innate, unconscious activities in which we witness the natural movement of who you really are, being expressed without any judgment. Just pause for a moment and think how you doodle. Look for it in the next sections to find which dominant Energy Type captures your doodle. It's not 100 percent accurate, but it's pretty close. It was correct for me! We will also look at how the movement of the four Energy Types expresses in the way you walk, sit, stand, talk, and how you maintain your personal space, including which interior design elements you are drawn to.

Physical Features: The physical body is a manifestation of your inner essence. The vibration and movement of the four Energy Types are expressed and shaped in all your physical features. Most people are blended, showing lines and shapes of at least two or three Energy Types, but you do have a predominant expression that honors one of the four. The body—and the energy in it—does not lie! It is honestly expressing your true nature.

PART

Find Yourself in Here!

OKAY, HERE IS THE DEAL: You are going to see yourself in each Energy Type. That is because you have all four Energy Types in you. You are created from the four primary elements that influence the movement of each Energy Type. That is what makes you a whole person. But you dominantly express one of the four Types. I have not met one person yet who doesn't. Your secondary Energy Type does play a strong supporting role for most people.

I express a dominant TYPE 3^{SM} Energy with a strong secondary TYPE 4^{SM} Energy. The dominance of each of the Energy Types in my profile looks like this: 3, 4, 1, 2. I lead with my TYPE 3^{SM} expression and also have a lot of tendencies that are influenced by the nature of my secondary TYPE 4^{SM}. My TYPE 1^{SM} Energy really comes out when I am having fun with my dominant TYPE 1^{SM} family members and friends. TYPE 2^{SM} Energy is the least expressive in me, but it is definitely expressing in me as I take care of the details of my life (I just don't fuss over them too much).

YOU ARE UNIQUE

Not everyone exhibits the same level of movement within each dominant Energy Type. There are levels within each dominant Energy Type. Some people have stronger expressions of their dominant Energy Type's movement. They are what I call a textbook, classic example of their Type's tendencies. Others express a dominant

Energy Type that is less prominent and more blended with their secondary Energy.

My youngest son Mario and oldest daughter Jenny are good examples of this idea. Mario expresses a dominant TYPE 1^{SM} Energy. His organization looks like disorganization to me. He is comfortable with loose ends in his life. He moves through life in a very random, cheerful way, with a strong belief that it is all going to work out and most of the time, he is right! His tendency for being so free of having any structure in his own movement has at times been a struggle for him in a world that demands a certain amount of predictability, follow-through, and order. He knows this about himself and seeks support from the people in his life who have the tendency and nature of structure to support him. He expresses his own unique level of TYPE 1^{SM} expression.

My daughter Jenny also expresses a dominant TYPE 1^{SM} Energy and she definitely expresses a fresh, buoyant, youthful, and playful energy. You can be certain that she will make a plan, then change the plan more than once as new possibilities constantly present themselves to her. She expresses her TYPE 1^{SM} nature differently in her manner of follow-through and commitment. She doesn't always follow through on everything she starts, but you can guarantee she will follow through on what is most important to her and her role as a wife and mother. Both of my children with dominant TYPE 1^{SM} Energy have different levels of expression.

"Before I discovered my true nature in the Energy Profiling course, I was a reserved, quiet woman who took a lot of criticism and bad treatment from everybody as I was afraid to speak out.

"I grew up in a family with a great rift between my mother and my father's side. My father's mother and aunt also lived with us. There were two factions. My younger brother Hein and I belonged to our mother's side and my youngest brother Norbert belonged

to my father's side, especially to my grandmother. I was a cheerful child and I often danced around and sang with joy.

"But this was not acceptable to my father's faction and the joy was literally beaten out of me. When my mother died after a four-year struggle with ALS, the light went out for me. (I was 14 then.) I had to cover up my joyful nature in order to survive in my father's faction. This is how I then became oblivious to my true inner nature.

"In June 2008 (at age 58), I did the Energy Profiling course and found that I was a TYPE 1^{SM} [Energy]. The one that lights up the room; the life of the party… Me? No way. But the more I thought about it in the ensuing weeks, the more I realized that I really was a TYPE 1^{SM}. I remembered who I truly was. I remembered the light and joy within me.

"As time has passed, the light within has been growing stronger and the joy, too. What a profoundly changing revelation it was for me. It changed my life!

"I am now more aware of my inner nature and do not tolerate bad treatment from others anymore. My relationship with my 18-year-old son has also changed for the better. The discord is gone. Now there is harmony. And a lot more fun! My friends have noticed the difference, too, as I am far more upbeat than before. I was even approached by a nice man the other day. This has not happened since my last relationship with a man 19 years ago, which resulted in my becoming a single mom.

"It is so fulfilling to live my true nature again. I am thrilled to be a TYPE 1^{SM} [Energy]. I would not have it any other way. I am truly grateful for this revelation through the Energy Profiling course. Thank you, Carol, for producing this wonderful course."

—HEDY KALKER (TYPE 1^{SM} ENERGY), GERMANY

Please understand that there are variables and levels of our dominant Energy Type. Just notice what your tendencies are and which Energy Type you see yourself as most. Assess more than your apparent personality traits and, most of all, follow your heart.

HOW TO RECOGNIZE YOUR ENERGY TYPE

There is no right way to find your natural self. Your path is perfect for you. For example, some of my clients say they just knew their Energy Type while reading a certain section of this book. Others have taken more time, considering all the information and using additional resources I have created (see the resource section in the back of this book). Ultimately, after some experimentation, it all worked itself out perfectly for them and it will for you, too.

It is possible that you had to hide your true nature in your childhood due to feeling unsafe or unacknowledged. Even though this might be the case, you will recognize the natural movement of your core true self in the following sections.

Fortunately, feeling confused about your Energy Type is a rare occurrence. I believe people innately know who they are, if they will tune in and honor their core true nature that expressed freely in their earliest childhood days. You might even want to look back to those days and notice what your movement was like as a child. Were you buoyant and bouncy, calm and serene, assertive and taking charge, or could you play well by yourself and sit still readily?

As you read, remember to look at these three primary areas of yourself to find your true nature:

1. Your inner expressions. This includes your thoughts and feelings, perceptions and values.
2. Your outer expression. This includes your gifts and talents, your personality traits, your body language and behavior tendencies.

3. The mirror. This includes your physical features and movement of your body lines.

Between 60 to 85 percent of what you read in the section on your dominant Energy Type should relate to you. The levels at which we express our dominant Energy Type will vary from person to person, and we must take into account the influence of our secondary energies. Together, these energies produce a unique expression of you. You will not match any given Energy TYPE 100 percent.

KNOWING YOUR ENERGY TYPE FREES YOU TO SUCCEED

Consider the possibility that you have misjudged your greatest gifts as your biggest weaknesses and your greatest physical features as flaws. It is not uncommon that after someone has discovered their Energy Type that they have one of the biggest Ah-ha moments of their life! They see that they perceived their natural movement and tendencies as flaws in their character. But then they realize that their innate gifts and talents that are influenced by their dominant Energy Type are really tremendous blessings.

What a relief! You no longer have to try to quiet and stop what is your God-given nature. I have come to realize my TYPE 3^{SM} Energy, my energy moves forward swiftly, pushing things and people to create outcomes. Yes, I can be experienced as forceful and intense at times, but the more consciously I manage my natural TYPE 3^{SM} movement in balance with the other Energy Types, I experience myself (and allow others to experience my gifts) in a balanced way. I have realized that trying to stop or slow my natural movement would be as easy as stopping Niagara Falls!

I use the following metaphor any time I start to judge my natural qualities in a negative manner. I now compare that kind of negative judgment to standing on the banks of the Niagara River saying:

"Knock it off, Niagara Falls. You're just way too pushy. Can't you just calm down and be more like the Mississippi?"

Read each section on the dominant Energy Types and see yourself in the one you have the most connection with. Have fun with this, enjoy yourself, and notice when you begin to put judgments and labels on what you are learning about. After all, it is all just vibration and movement supporting us in expressing who we truly are.

Remember that everyone has the right and opportunity to be successful, prosperous, happy, fulfilled, creative, generous. In all the qualities we strive for in our human experience, it is our dominant Energy Type that makes us different in the way we move and express our true nature in pursuit of these ambitions.

THE DOMINANT TYPE 1^{SM} PERSON

Primary Movement: *Upward, Light*
Natural Gift: *Ideas*
"I have a new idea, and we can do it!"
Dominant Quality: *Cheerfully lifting us up to feel more fun and hope*

TYPE 1^{SM} ENERGY IS NITROGEN/AIR. Its natural primary movement is upward and light. If you express a dominant TYPE 1^{SM} movement, you have an upward, light energy. You are inspiring, fun-loving, and hopeful. Your dominant physical features express animated shapes like a circle, heart, or the points of a star, visible in the eyes, the cheeks, and the overall body and facial shape.

TYPE 1^{SM} Energy is an extrovert expression, moving upward and out to create in this world. You have the highest level of natural movement of all the Energy Types. This natural high-level, upward, light, buoyant, random movement can be consistently observed through aspects of your human experience.

Other key words that describe the movement of a dominant TYPE 1^{SM} Energy are: fresh, youthful, animated, bubbly, brilliant, radiant, connected then disconnected, crisp, fun, unstructured.

Due to the high movement that expresses itself spontaneously, you may have been told a lot as a child—and even in your adult life to "Settle down" or "Stop moving."

This energy is both yin and yang. The lightness and buoyancy is yin movement; the energy moving out and up to create is yang movement.

Your energy is like the sun shining brightly or a burst of fresh blossoms on a cherry tree. You truly are a "breath of fresh air," just like your dominant Energy Type—nitrogen/air!

Keeping life light and fun is a primary motive for a TYPE 1^{SM} person. Most cultures have labeled this movement as a childlike expression and only acceptable when we are at a party, taking a break, or on vacation. We have perceived it as a movement that we grow out of when we become adults, and that to be successful in life we have to move through life more seriously. This is not true. Type 1^{SM} Energy is always light, fresh, and fun, no matter the age of the person. In fact, it is critical that a TYPE 1^{SM} person come up with a way of approaching the activities of life (whether it be work or play) in a manner that makes them more fun and light.

My daughter Jenny (TYPE 1^{SM} Energy) has found many ways to add this element of fun to her day-to-day life experience. She realized using a paper day-timer or electronic handheld PDA was not fun for her. To organize her life each week, she draws up her weekly calendar with all her commitments on a piece of paper, and fills the paper with animated pictures, which she then puts on the refrigerator. She shares, "Having the animated doodles and pictures helps me feel like what I have to do can be fun and light."

_____

"When I first heard about Carol Tuttle's Energy Profiling course I was curious to know more but not really enthused. I assumed it was like the many other personality tests I have taken over the years that attempt to classify people by everything from colors to seasons to star signs and alphabet soup. So I was very surprised to find that it really isn't like any other program I know

of—and the best part is that it has made a significant difference in the way I see myself and others.

"Once I discovered and accepted the fact that my leading Energy Type is a 1 (and I admit I came kicking and screaming to that conclusion!), I was able to see very clearly how the strengths and weaknesses of 1-ness have played out in my life. I now know why I love starting projects but not finishing them, and I have a much better sense of which complimentary Energy Types can help me be more effective in managing my business and life in general.

"The Energy Profiling program provides so much insight into relationships. One of the first things I did after being profiled was call my business partner—who I'm quite sure is a dominant TYPE 4^{SM} *[Energy]—and laughingly acknowledged that I must drive her crazy sometimes, and now I know why!*

"I have seen many relationship revelations come about in my family as my children have been profiled. The result is always positive and leads to a great deal of acceptance and understanding— of each other and of ourselves.

"Without a doubt, the Energy Profiling system is one of the most direct, easy to understand, and user-friendly programs I have ever used, and I do use it every single day. Thanks, Carol and company, for making it available."

—MARCY BROWN (TYPE 1^{SM} ENERGY), UTAH

NATURAL GIFTS AND TALENTS

TYPE 1 Energy initiates the cycle of wholeness by coming up with new ideas and the inspiration and hope of making them come true. Animation creates new life, and TYPE 1^{SM} Energy creates new life.

If you put this into a phrase, your phrase would be, "I have a new idea, and we can do it."

You truly do believe in the possibility of all your ideas. You can expect that TYPE 1^{SM} Energy will produce more ideas than you will ever be able to accomplish. When an idea or impulse of a new possibility comes to you, you immediately believe in it. You readily express your ideas in a way that enables you to see others believing in you and the idea. Because you always have more ideas than can be executed—and you will naturally become distracted by other new ideas as they pop up—other people may become confused and frustrated when it appears to them that you have dropped the ball.

People with dominant TYPE 1^{SM} Energy move through life like a bouncing ball. You take the ball and run with it, and you can also drop some balls along the way since you create too many new balls to juggle. Your primary shape is a circle, the shape of a ball. People can see the bounce of the ball in your movement from point A to point B. Like TYPE 1^{SM} Energy, a ball can bounce off its surface from any possible angle, in any possible direction! One of your dominant shapes in your facial features is a circle or the shape of a ball.

You are naturally optimistic, and you look at everything from the bright side. You are like the sun, shining brightly on humanity with a bright, brilliant nature or disposition. The shape of the sun is also a circle. Of any Energy Type, you are the most able to overlook difficulties and believe in the possibility of success. If you fail, you do not worry about it for long, but console yourself quickly and move on.

Ideas come easily and readily to you. Your natural movement of being light and carefree can keep you from following through and finishing things. Your constant challenge is execution and bringing your idea to the final outcome. My daughter Jenny (TYPE 1^{SM} Energy) shares, "I have great, big ideas, some of them elaborate ideas, but I know I benefit from getting help to make it all work, to make a plan and to execute the big ideas."

You are keenly alive in your environment and, of all the Energy Types, you are the most able to experience the present moment of your life.

The resilience of people with dominant TYPE 1^{SM} Energy is amazing. My youngest son, Mario (TYPE 1^{SM} Energy), came into our family when he was 15. He had experienced a difficult childhood of neglect with no stability and support. He was moved from place to place every couple of years throughout his childhood. His natural ability to connect and disconnect with his environment and the people in it supported him to more readily adapt to these frequent changes. He has remedied his relationships with his birth family, and due to his TYPE 1^{SM} nature, he can adapt with the two families he has and feel a connection with both of them. When he is with us, he connects with us; when he is with his birth family, he just as readily connects with them. His ability to thrive now as a young adult, due to his resilient, bright, cheery nature, is a gift. He is everyone's best friend and is always a pleasure to have around.

Important: It is important that a person with TYPE 1^{SM} Energy have fun and keep it light. If you try and slow down your movement and move more deliberately through life, you will just be going through the motions, having lost your connection with your core, true nature. You will be out of balance with your upward, light energy if you try to create too much structure or try to slow down and be deliberate.

The same natural tendencies that are your gift and talents can also be a challenge in your life, causing imbalance and disharmony. When your dominant movement is taking over your life and is not balanced by the other three Energy Types that are also a part of your being, it can be a challenge being you!

Challenge: You can get stuck in the idea phase, bringing in more ideas than you can follow through with. You easily disconnect from one thing that is already in progress to start something new. You like the newness so you leave other things undone that have already been started.

Challenge: Because new ideas distract you easily, events and people—and you—create a tendency to not always follow through. Others may experience you to be fake, unbelievable, and not to be taken seriously.

I recently told my TYPE 1^{SM} daughter, "You need to allow for your randomness within a world that demands a certain amount of structure, and you need to follow-through on things that support your relationships and quality of life. Be more conscious of where you drop the ball, so it does not interfere with the harmony you desire in your relationships."

Challenge: Because you are so light, you have a tendency to make "light" of things that hurt you at a deep level. You may shy away from standing up for yourself, and speaking what is true for you when others feel differently. You may hold back and adapt to others continually and in this, lose yourself. This will cause your light to dim over time, and you will not know who you are as you continue to play roles that are not the true you.

PERSONALITY TRAITS

You like change and new experiences. You talk readily and easily to people. You like to keep things light and fun, encouraging and motivating others along the way. If someone is feeling down, you will easily encourage them, cheerleading them to feel better. You move forward with excited and hopeful determination, always making things fun along the way.

You are naturally cheerful and have an innate love of pleasure and fun. You do not like to be alone, you love company and amusement, and you want to enjoy life. You tend to have an elated spirit, you are not given to worry and anxiety, your nature is to be carefree. You are consistent in not being consistent, changing plans, and living your life with more abandon than structure. You are able to respond to changing situations spontaneously with an inspired perspective.

The dominant element expresses in you is nitrogen/air. Phrases commonly used to describe your personality are: "You are a breath of fresh air," or when it becomes a judgment, "You are such an airhead."

Many things which cause other Energy Types a great deal of anxiety and trouble do not affect TYPE 1^{SM} people, because you are an optimist and, as such, overlook difficulties and prefer to look at all of life from the sunny side. Even when you are exasperated and sad, you soon find your balance again. Your sadness does not last long, and gives way quickly to happiness. This sunny quality allows you to get along well, even with persons generally difficult to work with.

You are friendly in speech and behavior and can pleasantly entertain others by interesting narratives and witticisms.

> **Challenge:** When you have not followed through or have let someone down by not keeping your commitments and not communicating, you have a tendency to give yourself excuses and make up stories as to why you could not follow through. If a new point of view presents itself, you may readily upset plans that you had made previously. This inconsistency often causes people to think that the TYPE 1^{SM} person is flaky. You deny such judgments because, in your mind, there is a good reason for your change. You forget that at times it would be supportive to your relationships to consider other people's feelings and to look into and investigate the ramifications of your ideas before you start to execute them. As you are aware

that you are easily captivated by every new idea or mood, you need to more consciously manage what you have already committed to with other people.

Challenge: Before you have mastered one subject, your interest relaxes because new impressions have already captured your attention. You love light work, which attracts your attention, where there is no need of deep thought or great effort. You can be hard to convince that you may tend to be superficial about things—on the contrary, you imagine that you have grasped the subject wholly and perfectly. You are so good at convincing others, you convince yourself. The evidence will be seen in areas like school where grades are applied or jobs that require more structure, and any other aspects of life that have standards of measurement you have to apply to.

Challenge: In your enjoyment you can be very frivolous. You can be inconsistent at work or entertainment—you love variety in everything, like a hummingbird that flies from flower to flower or the child who soon tires of the new toy.

Challenge: Because you are so adaptable with your light, non-structured, airy energy, and you have a sunny nature that boosts others up, you have a tendency to consider what others want before you consider what you want. With this tendency of saying "What do you want?" to others, you may also be trying to avoid taking responsibility in case things don't work out. This may even develop into feeling like you need to ask for permission for anything you want. If this is happening to you, you have allowed your upward, light, airy energy to take over, losing yourself in your own carefree nature.

THOUGHT AND FEELING PROCESSES

Your thoughts and feelings are quick and spontaneous. You process information so quickly that others can perceive you as not thinking things through. You know quickly what is right for you. Follow your quick intuition and impulses to stay balanced in your life.

My son Mario (TYPE 1^{SM} Energy) and I were driving along in the car chatting about his future. Since he graduated from high school, he had been living a very spontaneous life, moving every few months and changing jobs often. He was close to turning 21 and was beginning to seriously consider his future. I had been feeling inspired to encourage him to go to college and that we would be willing to help him with this pursuit. I shared my thoughts with him, he paused for a moment, then very quickly replied, "That's what I want to do!" I asked, "Are you sure? You hardly even thought about it." He said, "I know I don't have to. I know it is right."

This was another opportunity to remind myself that those with TYPE 1^{SM} Energy think things through quickly and can appear to others to not take things seriously. To the rest of us it appears you would need to take more time to think it through, but with the radiant, light, brilliant movement you are supported with, you do not. If you express TYPE 1^{SM} Energy, it is common for you to feel you have to slow your energy down and change who you are to be taken seriously by others.

I have also discovered that a lot of men and women with TYPE 1^{SM} Energy have a tendency to wear a lot of black in an effort to be taken more seriously and not look so youthful and bright. Ironically, it only conflicts with their animated nature, making their Energy Type more pronounced and amplified!

If you express TYPE 1^{SM} Energy, you organize things quickly in your mind, but you may look disorganized to others. This is because both your movement and your approach to life is more random. You can juggle many things at once, so it all fits together for you. You have quick mental organization. You are highly intuitive and can sense possibilities that others cannot.

Challenge: Because you readily see what doesn't exist physically and express your belief in it, you can attract disbelief from others, which can cause you to doubt your own inspiration.

Challenge: Your high level of belief can cause you to be gullible and appear naïve to others. As you recognize your tendencies and honor your true nature, most of this will drop off in your life and you will be seen as ingenious!

COMMUNICATION

You value change, fun, and spontaneity in your communication. You love having fun while understanding and connecting with others.

Both dominant TYPE 1^{SM} women and men are the talkers of the four Energy Types. You like to talk, chitchat, and enjoy verbal interaction while doing things.

You can often interrupt or jump from topic to topic when you are in the middle of a conversation because you process information so much faster than other people do. My son Mario (TYPE 1^{SM} Energy) calls it his "brain-jumping process."

You speak what you are thinking almost instantly. You feel no need to sort it out before you spit it out! You are frank, talkative, social, and your emotions are readily expressed.

You relish good conversation, but can also go with the flow. You can chitchat superficially with the best of them. In your conversations, you can move from one idea to another so quickly, it appears random to others.

You like to change focus often and move from one thing to the next, taking a lot in. You have a high level of belief and like to share that and use it to encourage others.

Challenge: You can appear random and ungrounded to others, since you can change your mind effortlessly and agree with others easily. You have an opportunity to learn how to say what is true for you, be true to your intuition and inspiration, and stay in your own light, upward momentum without feeling either guilty or pushy about it. Speak your truth as quickly as you know it. Act on your first impulse and trust it.

I am a Senior at Snowflake High School and just turned 18!... In junior high, I struggled finding my true self, like so many others. I allowed my secondary to take over. I was very quiet and pushed around. Because of this, I also struggled to find my masculine expression. I saw myself as weak, small, skinny, wimpy, soft, too sensitive, and immature. I was not happy.

It got a little better as I grew and matured, but I still was not living my true self. Then, I discovered the Energy Profiling system the summer before my Sophmore year. It was sooooo validating. I realized my bright, fun, and animated energy. I was determined to live my true nature. I began dressing my truth, and I looked GOOD, if I do say so myself! :)

Like I said, it has been over two years, and I have loved every minute of it!!!!!! I LOVE myself and all of my talents. I have learned to profile my friends and teachers, and support them in their natural movements. Many of my friends have learned their types and some have started dressing their truth! It has been sooooo fun!

I am a light to those around me. I am told almost every day how good I look in bright, vibrant colors, or how happy I am. My friends see me as a positive influence and a beacon of FUN! I don't know where I would be with out this knowledge that you have most graciously provided! Thank you, Thank You, THANK YOU!

—LANCE MERRELL (TYPE 1^{SM} ENERGY), ARIZONA

BEHAVIORAL TENDENCIES

You move like a babbling brook, bubbling along buoyantly at a rapid pace, turning from one activity to another.

Relationships: You seek a wide and broad range of friendships. You are not selective or exclusive. You are not insistent upon acceptance of your ideas or plans. You agree readily with others' wishes, being compliant and adaptable.

Challenge: You are so adaptable you may lose yourself to others. You are especially vulnerable to losing yourself as you adapt to TYPE 3^{SM} and TYPE 4^{SM} Energy Types.

Social: You have an eagerness to participate with others, whether at work or play. To you there is no difference between work and play if it is light and fun and you can be sociable with others. You readily make acquaintances with other people. You are very communicative, loquacious, and associate easily with strangers.

At social gatherings, the best part for you is bouncing from room to room and person to person.

Timeliness: You have a tendency for being late. You are consistent in your lateness. If you get close to the agreed upon time to be somewhere, getting close feels like being on time to you. You tend to be late because of your nature of being distracted as you move from point A to point B.

Work: You excel in positions that require innovation, new ideas, intuition, creativity, fun, and a sense of freedom. You can concentrate on multiple tasks at one time, but remember you tend to leave tasks unfinished because you love the freshness of starting something new. The more you are aware of this tendency the more you can manage your natural movement to be a gift in your life rather than a detriment, especially if you can delegate the completion of tasks to others.

Money: You tend to be very carefree with your money. Because you are not deeply attached to anything, including money, you can see a lot of money come and go in your life. You are a generous person and because you love to light up someone's life, you easily share your money and goods with others to bring a smile to their face. You enjoy using your money in this way.

We were trying to teach our son Mario (TYPE 1^{SM} Energy), who was 16 at the time, how to budget his money and manage it. One afternoon, he came home from school and he said, "Mom, I have a confession to make. I did something really bad." My first assumptions were that he got in a fight or got into trouble at school, which I mentioned as I thought of them. He told me, "No, nothing like that. I went to the bank and withdrew $40. I was going to save $20 for some things I need to buy and donate $20 to the Primary Children's Hospital drive they are having at school. I am sorry, Mom, I couldn't help it. I gave all $40 to the children's hospital!" People with a dominant TYPE 1^{SM} Energy naturally connect and disconnect with money more impulsively than the other Energy Types. While this can sometimes be a challenge, Mario's example reminds me that this tendency can also be a great gift when it comes to being naturally generous.

Physical Activity: You prefer group activities, whether work or play, and are not easily satisfied with individual projects unless the project you are working on is motivated by doing something for someone else. My daughter Jenny (TYPE 1^{SM} Energy) told me she is extremely motivated to finish things that she is doing for other people because she loves to see the smile on their face when she shares it with them. When you are exercising, you prefer to socialize at the same time and prefer group sports to individual sports.

BODY LANGUAGE

You may or may not have a predominant amount of TYPE 1^{SM} Energy expressing through your body language and physical features. Most people are blended in their physical features, so you won't see yourself in all these expressions, but you will notice many expressions of TYPE 1^{SM} body language and physical features if you are a dominant TYPE 1^{SM} person.

Walking: You walk with a buoyant, bouncy spring in your step.

Sitting/Standing: You sit and stand with a lot of movement, shifting your position often. You can appear to be restless and fidgety to others, as you do not like to sit or stand still, focusing on one thing for very long. You often sit with your legs crossed, what we call Indian style, or very comfortably on the floor.

Voice/Language: A TYPE 1^{SM} voice is a higher pitch and can even sound squeaky. It is an animated voice, or like a child's. When you answer the phone, even though you are an adult, and people are still saying, "Can I talk to your mother?" then you have a TYPE 1^{SM} voice!

Due to your bubbly, buoyant nature, when you speak, the tone of your voice rises and falls a lot. You speak with more dramatic, expressive, descriptive, animated language, and a lot of laughter. You always talk with your hands—actually, your whole body will be involved in expressing what you are saying. You like to use animated words and descriptions. Rachael Ray, a popular American TV show host, is a perfect example of TYPE 1^{SM} language. She does a lot of cooking on her show and she uses animated words like delish or yum-o, and uses acronyms like EVOO for Extra Virgin Olive Oil, and calls a sandwich a sammie all through her show. My TYPE 1^{SM} friend Lori ends her phone conversations with me using expressions like "See you later, Toots!" It works when she says it due to her animated nature; but if I were to say it, it would sound goofy!

Giggling is common for a TYPE 1^{SM} person, but you may not notice your tendency for giggling throughout the day or when you are talking to someone. Something else you may do that you have not noticed is using the phrase, "Just kidding!" frequently. My daughter Jenny (TYPE 1^{SM} Energy) says this immediately after she has teased someone or said something lightly sarcastic.

Doodling: You doodle using shapes that represent your natural movement—circles, stars, and hearts—with repetition that creates a feeling of animation, youthfulness and liveliness. For illustrations of TYPE 1^{SM} doodles, please visit www. myenergyprofile. com/doodle.

Personal Space: You like to keep things in sight, out, and around. You can be messy and appear disorganized to others. You would really rather not have to take the time to clean up. You figure you can do it later, or just do it real quick, so you can go do something more fun. If you create ways to make cleaning fun, it is more interesting to you.

Due to your very quick and spontaneous thought process, you have a tendency to misplace things, car keys being one of the most common items. You also frequently lose track of glasses, wallets, and purses. You are already on to your next thought, and will not pay attention to where you put your keys. Jenny knows her tendency for this pattern and now consciously puts her keys in the same place or even has a few backup sets to cover herself when she doesn't remember to put the keys in the designated place.

When you travel, it can be a challenge to narrow down your clothing choices, so you tend to bring a lot of clothes on your trip to give yourself plenty of options.

Interior Design: You like a lot of decoration. You have the highest movement in your being of any of the Energy Types, so seeing that high level of movement in your physical surroundings is very comfortable to you. You like things out where you can see them. You have a lot of fun with decorating for holidays, especially Halloween! I have not yet met a TYPE 1^{SM} person that does not like Halloween. It is common that it is their favorite holiday. Everything about Halloween screams TYPE 1^{SM}—the dressing up, the trick-or-treat theme, the candy, the spoofing—all are animated and fun.

PHYSICAL FEATURES

The overall quality of your physical expression is animated, youthful, and cute. Your bone structure creates circles and points of a star with your features being asymmetrical or random. For visual examples of TYPE 1^{SM} facial features, please visit www.myenergyprofile.com.

Skin and Skin Texture: TYPE 1^{SM} skin is fresh and youthful. The random nature of TYPE 1^{SM} movement is expressed in the skin as a combination skin with random dry and oily spots. Freckles, small moles randomly on the skin, blemishes and reddening (blushing) of the skin are all TYPE 1^{SM} skin features. You want a skin care product that helps you maintain the youthful, fresh appearance that's natural to your TYPE 1^{SM} skin.

Face Shape: Circular or heart shaped.

Cheeks: Circles, what we call "apple cheeks." Dimples are a TYPE 1^{SM} feature.

Nose: A circle shape on the tip of the nose or what we call a button nose. TYPE 1^{SM} Energy moves upward, so a turned-up nose is a TYPE 1^{SM} nose. A TYPE 1^{SM} nose also tends to be smaller in size.

Eyebrows: Come to a point right over the eye, or is half a circle.

Eyes: Round, pop out, with a sparkle or light in the eyes. A unique TYPE 1^{SM} feature is what we call "smiling eyes." When a TYPE 1^{SM} person smiles, their whole face smiles with an upward, light movement. Even your eyes and the lines on the sides of your eyes move upward when you smile.

Hands: Cherub-looking, chubby fingers, with a small, youthful appearance. Short fingers, short nail beds, and nails that can be circular or turn upward.

FAMOUS PEOPLE

Women: Sarah Palin, Sally Field, Doris Day, Reese Witherspoon, Drew Barrymore, Katie Couric, Rachael Ray, Dolly Parton, Shirley Temple, Meryl Streep, Goldie Hawn, Paula Abdul, Katie Holmes

Men: Johnny Carson, Will Smith, Jim Carrey, Will Ferrell, Adam Sandler, Jack Black, Ron Paul, Nick Cannon, Billy Crystal, Eddie Murphy, Jackie Chan, Chevy Chase, Martin Short

MUSIC AND MUSICIANS

Music that has high movement, is bright, buoyant or uplifting, is TYPE 1^{SM} music. A notable example is "Flight of the Bumblebee" by Nikolai Rimsky-Korsakov. Big Band style music is also TYPE 1^{SM} music. A few TYPE 1^{SM} musicians include Colby Coillat, Bob Marley, Michael Bublé, ABBA, Britney Spears, The Foundations, and Nelly Furtado.

NATIONS

The state of Hawaii in the U.S., and the countries Mexico, Tonga, Samoa, and Jamaica are all TYPE 1^{SM} locales and are the places where we like to go on vacation and play!

HOW YOUR ENERGY AFFECTS OTHER PEOPLE

Your energy creates an ambience of youthfulness and fun. Your upward, light energy lifts people around you. You are naturally a light to the rest of us. At times, your high level of movement can get annoying and feel intrusive to other Energy Types, especially a dominant TYPE 4^{SM} person. One of our clients who expresses a dominant TYPE 1^{SM} Energy shared, "As a business owner, I have the opportunity to deal with a lot of different people. Now I know why I annoyed some people and they did not take me seriously in my role. I am especially aware when I am interacting with a TYPE 4^{SM} person to tone my oneness down a bit and respect their needs. This has allowed me to create some fabulous business opportunities that I may not have been able to create if I had come off too random and playful."

As you are conscious of your natural movement and are more aware of who you interact with, you will be able to manage yourself in a way that supports others in being in rapport with you. As you stay conscious of who you are and love who you are, rather than judge your natural movement and try to silence it, you will consistently align with your core, true nature and others will always enjoy being around you.

FOR OTHERS: CREATING A SUCCESSFUL RELATIONSHIP WITH A DOMINANT TYPE 1^{SM} PERSON

DOs

Honor their animated nature by joining in with them. Let them help lighten things up for you. Know that their true nature—the natural movement expressed through them—is light, upward and uplifting!

Praise them and thank them for their ideas, even if they do not execute them. Don't make their follow-through your business. If you have the thought, "Yeah, I will believe it when I see it," catch yourself and think instead, "It is not my business what they do with their ideas. I think it is so great that there is always newness and freshness whenever I am with this person." A new idea can just be another option. TYPE 1^{SM}s are not strongly attached to their ideas, so it is not a big deal to tell them you have other plans.

Just as I was writing this, my son Mario called me. It is Christmas Day 2008. He was at the Salt Lake Airport getting on a plane to fly to Hawaii to meet the rest of the family that is already there.

He called and said, "Mom, I have an idea. Let's go to the movies when I get in." Well, I am already in Hawaii with the rest of the family, and some of them are different Energy Types. With three TYPE 4^{SM}s and three TYPE 2^{SM}s who have already created a plan and structure for the day, suddenly changing the plan to go to the movies was not a great idea! I told Mario the plan and he was fine with it. I neglected to say, "Mario that is a great idea. Thanks for sharing it. I love your ideas." I just went right to sharing the existing plan. He somewhat down-heartedly said at the end of the conversation, "Well, I just thought it might be a good idea." If I had praised his idea, it wouldn't have mattered so much if we didn't go to the movies. What mattered was that praising him for his true nature, a young man with many fun, even brilliant ideas and a great amount of love to share.

Laugh with them. Being with a TYPE 1^{SM} person is permission to let your hair down and have some fun. Know that their true nature—and the natural movement expressing through them—is light, upward, fresh, buoyant, animated, and new! As you accept that, you accept them.

Support a TYPE 1^{SM} person in following through on what they agreed to do when it involves you. Don't use the excuse, or let them use the excuse, that it's just their tendency to drop the ball as they come up with a good story along the way to justify it. We support their lack of structure in their own essence by offering the structure we naturally have in our essence to create balance in our relationship together.

Keep telling them they are cute or fun! They may get tired of hearing it, but like I tell my very cute adult daughter Jenny, "You are just cute, and it's a great thing!" For both TYPE 1^{SM} men and women, it's very validating of their nature to hear: "You are so much fun!"

DON'Ts

Don't judge them to be flighty and uncommitted. It is their light, upward energy you are experiencing. Don't say things like, "I can't take you seriously," or "Settle down," or "Stop moving," or "You're too old for that!"

Don't set yourself up to be disappointed by placing your expectations of how you (in your Energy Type) would move through life, and what you would do to get from point A to point B. It will not look the same for a TYPE 1^{SM} person, and it will probably never look the same twice!

While walking on the beach on a recent trip to Hawaii to visit our family home, my daughter Jenny lamented her own personal struggle of being a dominant TYPE 1^{SM} Energy. She was not allowing herself to be who she is and this trip was providing a lot of reminders of how she was not. She got headaches on a daily basis the first few days we were there. She realized her headaches were an indicator to her that she was trying to conform to be someone she was not. She was judging her light, airy ways as weak and immature. She was even bothered by the sun coming out every day and shining brightly on us! She made me laugh when she shared, "Mom, I was even mad at the sun for being so bright and shiny. It just kept reminding me that I was not living true to myself, thinking I need to be more serious and deliberate in my approach to life." She jokingly started shaking her fist at the sun, saying, "How dare you be so bright and warm. You better just knock it off, sun. You are really starting to get to me!"

Jenny once again committed to be her TYPE 1^{SM} animated, fresh, light self. At the end of our walk, she had an impulse to run into the ocean with all her clothes on and just go for a swim right then and there. She told me right before she took off, "I need to follow this impulse just to honor myself right now." It was a lot of fun to watch her skip off into the water!

SUMMARY OF THE DOMINANT TYPE 1^{SM} PERSON – UPWARD LIGHT ENERGY

Nitrogen/air is TYPE 1^{SM} Energy. A TYPE 1^{SM} has an upward, light energy. You are inspiring, fun-loving, and hopeful. Your dominant shape in physical features is the circle and points of a star and is most visible in the eyes, the cheeks, and the overall facial shape.

As you express your dominant TYPE 1^{SM} Energy, you may have a tendency towards these strengths:

- You light up the room when you enter and are often the life of the party.

- You have an optimistic attitude and can see the silver lining even on a cloudy day.

- You have the ability to multi-task extremely well, and you can jump from one idea to another in the blink of an eye. Others may find it difficult to keep up.

- You have many ideas and can think outside the box. When brainstorming, you may come up with the most ideas and the most creative ways to achieve them.

- You are light-hearted and have an innocence about you that attracts others.

- You look for fun ways to accomplish the things you want to do. Somehow, you can make any job seem fun.

- You are gifted with a brilliant mind that can organize many ideas, events, and schedules and move forward with them quickly and efficiently.

- Your ability to organize things in your mind so quickly and follow through may not appear to be organized to someone who moves forward in a linear pattern.

- Your energy is light, scattered, and upward. It is random in movement and appears to be unstructured and inconsistent to others. This allows you the ability to be flexible, change directions, and be open to new possibilities.

As you express your dominant TYPE 1^{SM} Energy, you may a tendency towards these challenges:

- You may have so many ideas that you become over-whelmed with the possibilities.

- You may choose not to do tasks that are undesirable because they are not fun.

- You may move, talk, or act before thinking.

- You may become too scattered or random to accomplish tasks in an orderly manner.

- You may be too light about situations and appear insincere or without thought.

TYPE 1^{SM} WORD PORTRAIT

Active	Daring	Impulsive
Adventuresome	Delightful	Industrious
Agreeable	Eager	Infectious
Airy	Easy going	Informal
Amenable	Effervescent	Ingenious
Amusing	Empathetic	Innocent
Animated	Enchanting	Inspiring
Anticipating	Encouraging	Intelligent
Asymmetrical	Energetic	Inventive
Awakening	Engaging	Irresistible
Beaming	Enthusiastic	Jovial
Bouncy	Exciting	Joyous
Bright	Exhilarating	Jubilant
Brilliant	Expressive	Laughing
Buoyant	Exuberant	Light
Candid	Festive	Light-hearted
Carefree	Flexible	Lively
Charismatic	Frank	Lovable
Charming	Fresh	Lyrical
Cheerful	Friendly	Magnetic
Cheering	Frivolous	Melodramatic
Comical	Frolicsome	Merry
Congenial	Fun-loving	New
Coy	Funny	Open
Creative	Generous	Open-hearted
Crisp	High-spirited	Open-minded
Curious	Idealistic	Optimistic
Cute	Imaginative	Outgoing
Dainty	Impudent	Outspoken

Permissive

   Pert

   Playful

   Pleasing

   Positive

   Precocious

   Quick-moving

   Quick-witted

   Radiant

   Random

   Rapturous

   Receptive

   Refreshing

   Renewing

   Restless

   Resilient

Scattered

Self-starter

Sense of being alive

Shining

Simple

Sincere

Social

Spirited

Sporadic

Sprightly

Sweet

Tenacious

Trendy

Twinkling

Uncomplicated

Unexpected

Unpremeditated

Upward

Vibrant

Vital

Vivacious

Vivid

Warm

Witty

Youthful

Zestful

The Dominant TYPE 2^{SM} Person

Primary Movement: *Fluid, Flowing*
Natural Gift: *Details*
"What do we need to know and do to make the idea possible?"
Dominant Quality: *Calmly connecting us to our hearts and each other*

TYPE 2^{SM} ENERGY IS OXYGEN/WATER. Its natural primary movement is fluid and flowing. People with dominant TYPE 2^{SM} movement have a fluid, flowing energy. You are calming, inviting, subdued, and sensitive. Your dominant shapes in physical features are elongated S curves, ovals, and softened rectangles, which are visible in the eyes, the nose, the cheek, the hairline, and overall body and facial shape.

TYPE 2^{SM} Energy is an introvert expression moving in a subtle and connected flow to create in this world. TYPE 2^{SM} Energy expresses as a medium-to-medium-low movement. This naturally subdued, connected, flowing movement can be consistently observed through aspects of your human experience.

Other key words that describe the movement of this energy in a dominant TYPE 2^{SM} person are: blended, soft, subtle, steady, easy-going, relaxed, connected, nurturing, comforting, warm, detail-oriented.

Due to your medium-to-medium-low movement that expresses itself calmly, you may have been told a lot as a child and even in your adult life to "Hurry up!" or "Make up your mind!"

Your energy is a double yin. Your softness and fluidness is yin movement. Your energy moves inward in an inviting manner to create, which is also yin.

Your energy is like the afterglow of the sunset or like dusk before the moon rising, creating an ambience of grace, softness and comfort. Your presence adds refinement and grace to the earth. Being in your presence helps us slow down and experience calmness in life. You truly are steady and easy-going, just like the Mississippi River, which is your dominant Energy Type oxygen/water!

Making sure life is comfortable for yourself and others is a primary motive for a TYPE 2^{SM} person. Comfort is a priority in every aspect of your life. Acting appropriately so as not to cause any discomfort for others, wearing comfortable clothing, sitting on comfortable furnishings, enjoying comfortable relationships, consuming comforting food, sharing comfortable communication— you name it, comfort is a priority. I have yet to meet a person with dominant TYPE 2^{SM} Energy who did not have comfort as their number one priority when it came to choosing an article of clothing.

As a TYPE 2^{SM}, you like to touch soft, smooth textures. For example, walking down an aisle in a clothing department, you run your hand along rack of clothes just to feel their softness. You love to touch baby's skin, puppies, kittens, or stuffed animals, and you gravitate toward luxuriously soft furniture or bedding. Here is a case in point: One day, my husband Jonathan (TYPE 2^{SM} Energy) returned home from shopping having bought himself a new fleece pullover. He enthusiastically took his new pullover out of the bag and called me over to feel how comfy it was. With my dominant TYPE 3^{SM} Energy, I did not relate to the value of comfort that he was experiencing and realized that this difference was being created by our very different natural expressions.

"My Energy Profiling story is not one with a huge, dramatic change, but rather one with more of a simple course correction...

"I was going along okay, but I didn't know what I needed to do to reach out for the unspeakable happiness I knew was out there for me. Now, I'm sure I'll find it.

"I feel that the timing was just right for me to discover the principles in Carol's book Remembering Wholeness... For some reason, I felt a strong desire to make a 10-hour trip to Denver, Colorado, from Midland, Texas, when no one else could go with me. When I was still determined to go, my husband made arrangements to accompany me. Then a friend I thought I just might have time to stop and see for a few minutes invited us to spend both of our nights in her home. Surprisingly, we did. It turned out that she was the one who gave me her copy of Remembering Wholeness to read on our return. I loved the book and found it comforting as well as enlightening. I was drawn to the truths in the book and to Carol herself.

"Seeking more, I searched her website. I was instantly intrigued, because I knew I wanted the insights and helps that were promised... As an older, middle-aged woman, I had learned a lot about relationships through trial and error, as well as study, and I had pretty much given up on books and tests, and their ability to work the magic I wanted. Things were going fine in my marriage and family, but I still had not come to the point of totally accepting myself. We were getting by, but the true companionship I sought with my husband eluded me. I didn't know how to communicate with him as I needed to. I thought it would be worth whatever I had to do to learn this information, if the claims were true.

"I was right. The knowledge I gained was richly rewarding...

"I [express a dominant TYPE 2^{SM} Energy], and I feel good about that, but I used to be confused about it. I always felt that I *needed to be stronger in some ways to balance my personality or something. I thought I was supposed to have some hardness, too. I was happy to discover that my questioning nature, compassion, and softness did not need to be changed to a more determined, assertive abruptness in order to be my best self. These are traits I thought my TYPE 3^{SM} husband would like because they are what I see in him.*

"I learned I should relax and concentrate on being the best I can be of what I really am. I would do better to be more compassionate with my husband (not expecting him to change to be more like me), directing my flow of questions into a different path, waiting patiently until he is ready for my softness, and so on. How wonderful it was, coming to understand him and know that in times past, his ways of doing things (that I judged as undesirable) were not necessarily unfeeling, inconsiderate, or too aggressive! I can now more easily accept and admire him the way he is, without fear that the traits I see in him will change and become too big for me to handle. My fears were based on groundless old ideas.

"I appreciate the understanding I have gained for my eight children and 10 grandchildren, too. I can see how beneficial it would have been to have this knowledge while our children were in our home. I have tried to become more accepting of them over the years and the Energy Profiling program helps a great deal in that regard.

"I grew up with a submissive attitude, and the feeling that my self-esteem would be strengthened if I got good grades and did everything others expected of me. It was hard for me to be sure my own ideas were worthwhile. While that assessment did improve somewhat as years went by, knowing my Type has made a big difference in how I feel about myself. I haven't reached my destination yet. I am still evolving and trying to incorporate these truths into my life. But I am extremely grateful for the bits of knowledge

that have made my course corrections possible. I proceed with anticipation and expectations of joy.

"My husband is nearing retirement, and as we make plans for our new future, I am truly excited about the prospects of spending so much more time with him than ever before!"

—DARLA BUSHMAN (TYPE 2^{SM} ENERGY), TEXAS

NATURAL GIFTS AND TALENTS

Once the idea has been created—which is initiated by the natural gift of TYPE 1^{SM} Energy—the natural gift of a TYPE 2^{SM} becomes the next phase of the cycle of wholeness by starting the process of asking questions to gather the details. Your energy creates connection and flow. If you put your natural gift into a phrase, your phrase would be, "What do we need to know and do to make the idea possible?"

It is necessary for you to ask the questions and lead out with a degree of skepticism. This supports your need to question if the possibility could become a reality.

Once the details have been gathered, a person with TYPE 2^{SM} Energy can move forward, figuring out the steps to create a plan that will flow. This process is a tremendous gift to help us gather, organize, and flow the details which are necessary to make an idea a reality.

Important: Asking questions and gathering details is so prominent in your natural expression that it is necessary for you to give yourself time to ask the questions and gather details. Once you have gathered the details, you need to study those details and allow yourself time to process all the contingencies that you feel are valid in order for you to feel comfortable in making a decision and moving forward in your life.

Your sensitivity to details is a remarkable gift. You notice the details that make life flow more smoothly and comfortably for everyone else—like making things look nice, spending a little extra time on wrapping a gift, or presenting a meal you cooked. For example, my TYPE 2^{SM} mother never let us put the milk carton on the dinner table; instead, she insisted that the milk be poured into a pitcher and then put on the table so it would be more attractive!

When you share an experience or tell a story, you include a lot of details. You may notice that the stories in this book that are shared by TYPE 2^{SM} individuals include the most details and are the longest in length. It was common for the individuals who sent in the detailed stories to make an apology that it may be inappropriately long by including so many details!

You are the saints of the world. Without your gift of keeping us all connected at the heart, we may have annihilated ourselves as a planet by this time in history!

Growing up with a TYPE 2^{SM} mother was a great gift in my life. To be honest with you, I did not realize the gift my mother gave me and our entire family until I understood the nature of a TYPE 2^{SM} person. Prior to this understanding, I viewed my mother as somewhat of a doormat. I could not relate to how she managed her life. When I came to appreciate and understand that the nature of a TYPE 2^{SM} person is like a saint, I truly was humbled and even brought to tears of gratitude for the gift of my mother's 2-ness.

Because of the predominantly TYPE 3^{SM} and 4^{SM} Energy presence in our family (due to the Energy Types of my dad, brothers, and me), our home was often a very intense, competitive, harsh environment. It definitely lacked a playful, light mood since no-one in my family expressed a dominant Type 1^{SM} Energy. What I came to realize—once I understood the gift and power of TYPE 2^{SM} Energy—is that my mother was and is the reason we came through as a family. My mother's gift kept us all connected when many situations throughout the years could have caused us to disconnect.

You move through life like a deep, steady river. You are deliberate and methodical in your approach to life. My oldest son, Chris expresses a dominant TYPE 2^{SM} Energy with a strong secondary TYPE 4^{SM} Energy. Ever since Chris was a little boy, he has moved through life very subtly, very true to his TYPE 2^{SM} Energy, being keenly aware of what was going on around him, which is his TYPE 4^{SM} tendency. He often shares stories or makes comments in respect to events of his childhood that I had no idea he was paying any attention to, because as a child and young boy he never said anything about it!

As his TYPE 3^{SM} mother, I truly wish I had known his Energy Type when he was young. I would have stopped moving with such intense determination every day of my life and would have taken more time to just sit and be with him, quietly and comfortably. But as I teach in my book, *Remembering Wholeness*, it is never too late to be a good parent. So now, when I am with Chris, I choose to be sensitive to his subtle nature and pay keen attention to what he is sharing with me.

Your primary shape is an elongated S curve—the shape of a long winding river, moving deeply, steadily on its course. You can see the relaxed flow of the river in your movement from point A to point B.

One of the dominant shapes in your facial features is the elongated S curve, as well as the quality of being blended and subdued in your physical coloring.

You are naturally sensitive. Your softened, subdued movement enables alertness and creates this quality of sensitivity. You are sensitive to how people feel around you. You are sensitive if people feel uncomfortable, and you have a natural gift of inviting them to feel more comfortable. You are sensitive to details and plans. You can even experience sensitivity to foods, chemicals, electronics, and environments.

I recently asked a dominant TYPE 2^{SM} client, "Have you experienced any sensitivity to any of the products you have used in the past?" She shared with me her frustration at having what she judged to be overly sensitive skin. I explained to her that her skin's sensitivity was connected to the gift of her 2-ness—the gift of being sensitive and calm, of being aware of people and details, of helping us all feel connected and comfortable. I was not prepared for what happened next, since I thought we were just doing a simple skin profile. Suddenly, she burst into tears and buried her head in her hands. Through her joyful sobs, she shared with me that she finally got it! That what she had been deeming her weakness was actually her greatest gift. I sat there, amazed that such a simple interaction could call forth an innate understanding and validation for this woman. Wow. I was beginning to catch on that this Energy Profiling information was beautiful and powerful!

The same natural tendencies that are your gift and talents can also be a challenge in your life, causing imbalance and disharmony. When your dominant movement takes over, unbalanced by the other three Energy Types that are also part of your being, you can be challenged by being you!

> **Challenge:** You can get stuck in the investigation stage where, in asking questions and gathering details, you feel like you need to ask even more questions and gather more details before you can make a decision and move forward.

> **Challenge:** Your tendency to constantly ask questions and seek details can cause you to question yourself and not trust yourself and your decisions. Due to your more subtle movement, you are not as readily adaptable to change, which can turn into a fear of change.

> **Challenge:** You like to "fuss" over details. If this attribute is not channeled in a positive way, you tend to "fuss and worry" about life details, like money, health, relationships. Find a hobby that allows you to use this natural gift of paying attention to details so you can channel this energy into something that adds value to your life rather than cause you

to worry. My husband Jonathan (TYPE 2^{SM} Energy) realized his fussing over the details of our finances came from not channeling his gift for details into something else. He has taken up a couple of hobbies like wood carving and fly fishing which support him in flowing his attention to detail into something that is pleasurable to him rather than being excessively focused on the details of our finances.

PERSONALITY TRAITS

You have a great ability to help people feel connected due to your soft, gentle, relaxed, easy-going way. You encourage other people to relax and take it easy. You connect with people from your heart, which causes you to be very sensitive to how others feel. If someone is feeling down, you are sensitive to that without them even having to share it with you, and then you quietly help them feel better. You will reassure them that everything will be okay in a loving manner.

You move forward in your life with soft and quiet determination.

If you are challenged or dealt with too intensely, your tendency is to hold back or go within, feeling the need to retreat in some manner. You will then think about what you may have done to cause this response in another person, often assuming it was your fault.

Again, the dominant element that expresses in you is oxygen/water. Phrases commonly used to describe your personality: "You are so easy-going, you just go with the flow," or when it becomes a judgment, "You are so wishy-washy that you can never make up your mind." Your gift of going with the flow can turn into wishy-washiness, like the water that represents your energy!

Challenge: Your priority is not honor and recognition; your priority is to be appropriate to others so they feel comfortable with you. With this tendency, you do not give yourself enough credit when credit is due. Let yourself be in the limelight more often. You deserve it.

Challenge: Your personality is naturally sensitive. It would benefit you to pay close attention to your tendency to feel resentment, and potentially excessive sensitivity in the face of even small humiliations.

Challenge: You can judge your subtle, relaxed nature to be weak and wimpy. The next time you have that thought, just think of the Mississippi River or a mighty willow tree with deep roots and cascading branches and compare yourself to that movement. There is no weakness there, just a deep steady flow, knowing exactly where it is going, winding and bending as it flows along its way. Or think of the willow, standing elegantly in the breeze, offering comfort and support to anyone who sits under its shade to rest and relax for a while.

Challenge: Your softened, blended, muted energy can cause you to feel like you blend into the background, causing you to feel unimportant. You can feel overlooked and unnoticed.

I would like to point out that this section is the longest in the book! I wanted to honor those with TYPE 2ᔆᔉ Energy who submitted their stories by including so many of the details they beautifully shared.

"At first, it was very difficult for me to accept being a dominant TYPE 2ᔆᔉ [Energy] because it seemed so powerless. I was happy, however, to learn that I did not have to force myself to be friendly

and talkative to everyone I met. That is a talent of the TYPE 1ˢᴹ Energy!

"It was an incredible, amazing experience to embrace my true nature as a TYPE 2ˢᴹ [Energy]. In fact, it is hard to put into words the way it changed my life! I came to an understanding of myself that has changed literally everything in my life! I continue to be amazed at the transformation I enjoy and my life continues to transform into something more amazing all the time.

"The Energy Profiling system was the catalyst I was searching for—without even realizing I was searching—to discover my true inner self and let that shine! I love myself, I love my life and I am thrilled to know and live my true nature!"

—ROSS ANNE GIBSON (TYPE 2ˢᴹ ENERGY), IDAHO

THOUGHT AND FEELING PROCESSES

Your thoughts follow a steady stream that all connect and make sense. You want a lot of details so you can make these connections in your mind. You need questions answered and details gathered to make a decision. You like to put all the details together to see what the outcome could be. Change can be slower for you, while gathering of information and details and thinking it out thoroughly makes change an option. You like to think ahead and know where things are going.

You like your plans to follow a steady flow. You are not readily adaptable to change. You need time to ask questions and gather details and think things through. You cannot as readily disconnect from what your plan is to a new plan.

Your thoughts are slower and more methodical. You have a continuous process of interconnected thought. You tend to connect the past to the now which then connects to the future. Being told to just live in the now with no thought to the past or future would be a difficult challenge for you. My daughter Anne (TYPE 2ˢᴹ Energy) shares that she now understands the nature of her thoughts and just goes with the flow of them. When she was dating with the intent to meet someone and get married, she would go into great detail in her mind about where the relationship might go with every guy she went out with. One thought would lead to the next, which would lead to the next and the next, all the way to wondering if they would marry, how many children they might have, where they might live—and this was all being thought out in her mind before they even went on the date!

You have many fond memories and love reflecting on your memories. To maintain your connection to the past and your memories of it, you are inclined to create a connection to those memories through keepsakes, photos, scrapbooks and journals. Anne has faithfully kept a daily journal of the details of her life since she was in grade school.

> **Challenge:** You are a more methodical thinker that others may judge as slow. You feel it is necessary, first of all, to consider and reconsider everything surrounding a matter until you can form a calm and safe judgment.

> **Challenge:** Your attention to detail can turn into brooding, fussing, and worrying excessively. Of the four Energy Types, you are the worriers!

> **Challenge:** You can process information over and over in order not to leave anything out, which creates a tendency to get overwhelmed and find it hard to make a decision.

My daughter Anne (TYPE 2^{SM} Energy) and I were on our way to meet my other daughter, Jenny (TYPE 1^{SM} Energy) for dinner. My cell phone rang just as we arrived at our destination and Anne commented, "I bet that is Jenny and she hasn't left yet!"

Yes, it was Jenny and she hadn't left yet! People with dominant TYPE 1^{SM} Energy have a tendency to be late due to their tendency to get distracted easily. She was calling to offer us another possibility of where to go to dinner. She cheerfully made her suggestion, I told Anne about Jenny's new idea, and Anne replied, "No, I am not going anywhere else. I have already decided what I am going to eat, where we are going to sit, what we might talk about, I have it all planned out in my mind." I told Jenny, "No go. Anne has her mind set on this place."

Since Jenny's energy easily adapts and she is not deeply attached to her ideas, she was fine. As the mother of these two daughters, I was able to honor them both in that moment. I knew it would not offend Jenny to stay with our first idea and that she was just doing her job in offering another possibility. I honored Anne's TYPE 2ˢᴹ tendency for not being as easily adaptable and having a mindset that thinks things through with many details to consider. We ended up having a lovely evening enjoying each others' company, which includes our similarities and our differences.

Communication: You are slower in responding. If you are called upon to answer quickly or to speak without preparation, or if you fear that too much depends on your response, you become restless and do not find the right words and consequently often make a false and unsatisfactory reply.

You have a tendency to assume things and can act like you are correct in your assumption and proceed to respond to the people you are communicating with based on only your assumption. Rather than assume and move forward, share what you are assuming and communicate your assumptions to see how accurate they are. I learned this being married to a TYPE 2ˢᴹ husband for over 29 years—it just took me 28 years to notice it!

One day, during an emotional conversation with my husband Jonathan, I noticed him responding to me according to his unspoken assumptions about how I must be feeling about the topic at hand. Because I express TYPE 3ˢᴹ Energy with secondary TYPE 4ˢᴹ

Energy, my communication style is to the point and very black and white. I do not hold back. I say it how it is for me! I told him I do not say one thing, but really mean another. He responded to me by saying, "Really, you just say it straight out how it is for you?" I remarked, "Yes dear, you are the one who has the tendency to assume things, not me, I don't even have it in my thought processes to have to avoid it!" Knowing he has the tendency to assume things has helped Jonathan consciously manage this tendency to avoid unnecessary conflict by being more open and sharing his assumptions or even realizing many of them are unfounded since he now knows he can trust me to say exactly how I am feeling about something.

"My wife has been into your [Energy Profiling information] for about 6 months now. At first, I considered it another fad or gimmick, but I found myself fascinated by what I was hearing from her and the videos that she'd watch late at night in bed. I soon started to realize why it was fascinating: it actually made sense, it was truth. I came to recognize the resonating value: knowing yourself promotes confidence, a sense of peace, and the ability to harness your gifts.

But I've found that one of the most interesting uses of the principles is in identifying the various energies in others. This has happened at work, in church, and in my family. I am able to interact with others more effectively because I can perceive their motivators and the purpose/reasoning behind what they do or say. I feel like if I get good at this, I can become a sort of social skeleton key, being able to comprehend and even unlock people's personalities and have more meaningful interactions and relationships."

—ADAM MICHAELSON, UTAH

BEHAVIOR TENDENCIES

Your behavior tendencies express like a calm, steady river, moving along methodically in a relaxed, subtle manner following the plans you have made.

Relationships: You value emotional availability, consistency, fiscal responsibility, and accountability in your relationships. You have innate sensitivity to be appropriate so others feel comfortable around you. If I got loud or outspoken in a public setting, it would be common for Jonathan to shush me and tell me I was talking too loud. This used to cause me to want to react and get louder, but I now understand his tendency for not wanting to cause anyone discomfort.

Social: You are diplomatic, empathetic, proper, meticulous, preferring to observe rather than participate in larger social settings. You have an introverted energy. This does not mean you are shy. That is a label with a negative connotation. An introverted energy means that your energy expresses as an inward flow rather than an outward flow. Due to your soft-spoken nature, others may perceive you as shy. This always bothered my son Chris (TYPE 2^{SM} Energy). When he was judged as shy, he did not feel it was an accurate assessment of who he was. He now appreciates understanding his 2-ness and his more introverted soft nature that has nothing do to with his level of confidence and self-esteem.

In a social setting, you will be aware of the sense of community and connection that is occurring or not occurring. You are sensitive to how everyone connects and fits together as a group.

Timeliness: You tend to be on time due to your ability to make a plan and stick to it.

Work: You may appear to others to be slow at your tasks. Yet what you are really doing is working carefully and reliably, but only if you have ample time and are not pressed. You do not see yourself as a slow worker.

You will default to let others be preferred over you, even if they are less qualified and capable than your are in the particular work or position, but at the same time you feel slighted because you are being ignored and are assuming your talents are not appreciated.

Money: You are great with numbers and taking care of the details of managing money. Due to your meticulous nature and attention to detail, you are good with managing your money, but you can get bogged down by brooding, fretting and worrying about money concerns and having to know where every little cent is going.

Physical Activity: You typically plan out your exercise and fitness. You like to have a plan and follow it. You enjoy interacting with others on a more intimate level in your recreational and physical pursuits.

BODY LANGUAGE

You may or may not have a predominant amount of TYPE 2^{SM} Energy expressing through your body language and physical features. Most people are blended in their physical features, so you won't see yourself in all these expressions, but you will notice many expressions of TYPE 2^{SM} body language and physical features if you are a dominant TYPE 2^{SM} person.

Walking: You have a smooth, graceful walk. You take longer steps and keep your feet close to the ground. There is no bounce in your step, rather a very fluid flowing movement.

Sitting/Standing: You sit and stand in the shape of an S curve. A relaxed bend, holding your head to the side.

Voice/Language: You have a softer voice of medium pitch. You can be hard to hear at times. You may have been told you mumble! You use comforting, nurturing language. You speak in detail and ask many questions.

Doodling: You doodle in long S curves, ovals, and soft relaxed shapes, connecting the shapes together. For illustrations of TYPE 2^{SM} doodles, please visit www.myenergyprofile.com/doodle.

Personal Space: You are the pile makers. All your piles have a connection and you have an ongoing plan to get rid of the piles. And, when you do, it does not take you long to create new piles! When cleaning, you like to take more time to go through things in detail.

You like to keep things that connect you to the memories of the past. My daughter Anne (TYPE 2^{SM} Energy) has kept personal items all through her life from her baby blanket, to a favorite sweater from grade school, to making scrapbooks and taking a lot of pictures through the years, all to keep the connections of her memories going.

TYPE 2^{SM} men have a tendency to hang onto the large boxes that TVs, computers, and other electronic equipment come in. Both my TYPE 2^{SM} husband and son recently discovered this tendency. Their motive is, "Just in case I need it, I'm prepared!"

I also realized my husband has a tendency to own gadgets that have a lot of cords! He has more cords and cables, in piles of course, and I have no idea what they are for. I lovingly teased him that he must need all those cords to feel like he can keep things connected and plugged into his world!

Interior Design: Comfort is your number one priority in how you decorate your home. You like comfort in all things. Giving attention to detail in your décor and creating a soft, comfortable, cozy environment is right for you.

PHYSICAL FEATURES

The overall quality of your physical expression is softened and blended. Your bone structure creates elongated S curves and ovals.

Skin and Skin Texture: TYPE 2^{SM} skin is soft and supple with blended skin tones. It is free of wrinkles and lines and as a result, you look younger as you age. TYPE 2^{SM} skin drapes beautifully and softly over the bone structure. It is also typical that a dominant TYPE 2^{SM} person has a very low and subtle contrast in their skin and hair coloring. People with TYPE 2^{SM} skin maintain a soft, supple appearance to their skin, having the least wrinkles even as they age. My mother who has TYPE 2^{SM} skin does not look her age at all, due to her soft, supple skin. Due to your sensitive TYPE 2^{SM} nature, you may be sensitive to some skin care products. Embrace this gift of sensitivity and be patient as you find products that work for you knowing your sensitive nature is just expressing in your skin!

Face Shape: Oval

Cheeks: Long S curve, elongated cheek, or dropping cheek, hush puppy cheek.

Nose: Soft on top, medium size, S curve on side, S curve in the nostrils.

Eyebrows: Half of an oval, long S curve, very long eyebrows, not very high arch.

Eyes: Big, almond-shaped eyes, doe eyes, dreamy eyes, heavy-lidded or drooping eye lids.

Hands: Soft, graceful, smooth, long fingers that taper toward nail, oval nail beds.

FAMOUS PEOPLE

Women: Jane Seymour, Jaclyn Smith, Barbra Streisand, Angelina Jolie, Julia Roberts, Princess Diana, Grace Kelly, Shelley Long, Angela Lansbury, Jennifer Aniston, Emma Thompson, Viola Davis, Jennifer Hudson

Men: Richard Gere, Hugh Grant, Jay Leno, Steve Martin, Russell Crowe, The 14th Dalai Lama, John Krasinski, Bob Costas, Ryan Reynolds, Jerry Seinfeld, Warren Buffett, Mark Zuckerberg, Bill Gates

We love the TYPE 2SM men in chick flicks. With their genuinely soft and inviting nature, they always do well in romantic films.

MUSIC AND MUSICIANS

Music that has low movement and is calming and soothing is TYPE 2SM music. A notable example is Johann Pachelbel's "Canon in D Major." A few TYPE 2SM musicians include Jack Johnson, James Taylor, Imogen Heap, Damien Rice, Jewel, John Mayer, Sarah McLachlan, Azure Ray, and Natalie Merchant.

NATIONS

Thailand, Ireland, Australia, Tibet, and Canada are known for having very peaceful people and peaceful ways.

HOW YOUR ENERGY AFFECTS OTHERS

Your energy creates an ambience of calmness and connections. Your fluid, flowing energy relaxes people around you. You are naturally a calming influence to the rest of us. Others experience you as modest and humble. At times, your lower-level movement can feel slow and draining to others if you are not moving forward in your life, like a river with a log jam that is collecting debris and getting murky.

Your skeptical nature and need to ask questions can cause others to see you as a "doubting Thomas" or a "worry-wart."

As you are conscious of your natural movement and are more aware of who you interact with, you will be able to manage yourself in a way that supports others in being in rapport with you. As you stay conscious of who you are and love who you are rather than judge your natural movement and try to silence it, you will be consistently aligned with your core true nature and others will always enjoy being around you.

FOR OTHERS. CREATING A SUCCESSFUL RELATIONSHIP WITH A DOMINANT TYPE 2ˢᴹ PERSON

DOs

Give them the time they need to think things through. Allow them to ask questions and even encourage it. I now will say to my husband, "Do you have anymore questions you need to ask?" Recognize their gift for keeping us connected at the heart and their sensitive nature.

Know that their true nature—the natural movement that expresses through them—is subtle, blended, steady, connected, and relaxed! As you accept that, you accept them.

DON'Ts

Don't get pushy or demanding towards them. If you get loud, aggressive and pushy, a TYPE 2ˢᴹ person will just fade away. It is not in their natural movement to challenge this kind of energy coming at them. They will retreat rather than react.

Don't set yourself up to be disappointed by placing your expectations of how you (in your Energy Type) would move through life, and what you would do to get from point A to point B. It will not look the same to a TYPE 2^{SM} person. TYPE 2^{SM} people move very methodically, rarely detouring from their detailed plan.

"I thought about apologizing for a long story, but I am accepting myself [and my TYPE 2^{SM} Energy], and the fact that I tell things in detail!

"In March 2008, my sister called and asked if she and two of her daughters could stay with me for three days while they attended a class called Dressing Your Truth. I loved the idea of having my sister with me because we don't see enough of each other, and she is one of my favorite people. I decided that I would be able to spend more time with my sister and nieces if I attended the class with them. I signed up for the class with absolutely no idea of what I was getting into, other than the fact it was offered by Carol Tuttle! I just wanted to spend more time with my sister. My sister had introduced me to Remembering Wholeness by Carol several months previously, so I knew whatever the class was about, it would be compelling!

"Imagine my surprise when we arrived at the class, and found I was going to learn more about my energy/personality type, and how to support my true self. The idea of supporting my true self was very intriguing to me, because I had been praying for several months to change my thought patterns and heal myself from a pattern of anxiety and fear. I had made significant progress, but was feeling stuck again.

"As I began learning about the four different Energy Types, I immediately recognized that I had many characteristics of a TYPE 2^{SM} [Energy]. My thought patterns are very connected. I get very caught up in details. When someone proposes a project, my mind immediately jumps to the specifics of how we are *going to accomplish that task... I could relate to the idea that I am connected and comfortable. However, I was uncomfortable with many aspects of a TYPE 2^{SM}. I did not consider myself elegant, graceful, romantic, or even easy and relaxed. I remember thinking, 'I don't want to be subtle and blended. If I am a TYPE 2^{SM} [person], I might as well not exist, because no one will ever notice me. I will just blend in and disappear.' ...*

"I decided to have a positive attitude, and see if there was truth in this experience that I needed to learn. I immersed myself in the process... But on day three, I melted down. I found myself crying during the middle of our class. Learning all these new things about myself was very unsettling. I knew deep in my heart that I was a TYPE 2^{SM} Energy, but I still didn't want to be. I really felt that if I embraced being a 2, I would become lost to the rest of the world. No one would ever notice or see me. I realized I really hadn't accepted myself for who I am.

"I took the challenge given at the end of the class, and chose to exclusively dress like a 2 for three weeks. I have never looked back. I had lost 35+ pounds several months prior to attending the Energy Profiling class. Very few people had noticed. Once I began dressing my truth I had many, many people tell me how fabulous I looked and ask me how much weight I had lost recently!

"Knowing my Energy Type has been a life-changing experience for me. I have learned who I really am, and I love it! I love me! Having this knowledge about myself has validated me. Changing my outward appearance is only a tiny part of the changes I have experienced. In fact, it is probably the least important aspect of my transformation. I feel whole and complete now that I know myself...

"Finding out who I am has helped me personally, but knowing my Type has helped me even more profoundly in my relationships with my family. I took several of my children to an Energy

Profiling class, and have discovered the Energy Types of each of my five children plus my husband. I was very surprised to find I have some of each Energy Type in my family! I have gained a deep, enlightened view of my family members and how we relate to each other. I discovered where I have perhaps stifled a child because I put my expectations and thought patterns on them based on my Energy Type rather than theirs.

"My acceptance level and understanding of each of my children and spouse has grown immensely. We talk about the different Energy Types we each have, and how we express that energy in our lives. My children will be much more prepared to accept themselves, their spouses and their children, with the knowledge they have gained in their teenage years. We are growing closer as a family, and showing increased levels of Christ-like love for each other as we have come to accept each other as we are. We are realizing that we each have unique gifts and talents that come with our Energy Type. We do things differently, and have different thought processes, but we love each other even more as we truly understand each other."

—ANNETTE MYERS (TYPE 2^{SM} ENERGY), UTAH

"Several months ago, I came to your Energy Profiling class. All the information strongly indicated that I that I [expressed TYPE 1^{SM} Energy], or so I thought! Of course! Energetic, spontaneous, playful—that was me.

"I joined the chatty group of TYPE 1^{SM} women after the class and realized that I was the only one silent. I loved being in that group but as a listener and observer. Carol came up to me and assessed my physical features and said according to my Body Profile that I might be in the wrong group and to consider that I might be a TYPE 2^{SM} [Energy]!

"I was shocked. I did not enjoy the company of these gloomy self-absorbed individuals (or so I thought).

"TYPE 2ˢᴹ? I began rereading the tendencies for TYPE 2ˢᴹ Energy. I began thinking and questioning myself... I began to realize that I loved the company of TYPE 1ˢᴹs so much that I wanted to be one of them. I wanted to be energetic, spontaneous and playful. But in real life, I was not. It was quite a discovery. Slowly, I started to see the positive traits of TYPE 2ˢᴹ [people]. I stopped trying to be someone else and started to be more of who I really am. This process is not over yet, but what a journey! Thank you!"

—MILANA PEREPYOLKINA (TYPE 2ˢᴹ ENERGY)

(Note: Notice how many question marks Milana used in writing her story. How true to her TYPE 2ˢᴹ Energy!)

"In my mid-to-late 20s I went through a period where I thought I was maturing and growing up, but after going through the Energy Profiling course, I realized that I was actually changing from my true nature to that of one that was cultivated by my career.

"I am a TYPE 2ˢᴹ Energy that changed to my secondary 3, and lived that way for over a decade. I was pretty introverted when I started college and I soon found that the professors liked it when the students had input in the lessons. I started speaking up in class and pushing myself to voice my opinions. When I graduated from college, I went to work as an accountant for a construction company. Being female, it was hard for me to work in a primarily male environment. I had to push myself even more to overcome my shyness. The first couple of months the men that I worked with walked all over me. The company was not getting the results my managers expected of me. I was taught to be a forceful

person. I had to become very strong, very vocal, and very hard-nosed. I became known for my directness. They started calling me the 'Queen Bee,' sometimes as a compliment, sometimes not. I became very good at my job and respected for my abilities. I learned to live with the anxiety attacks that started plaguing my life. Xanax became a way of life for me. I couldn't understand why I felt uncomfortable in my own skin. I was successful, respected, and had a career that was fruitful. But why was I so unhappy?

"During this time, my 15-year marriage broke up. I blamed my ex-husband for changing and wanting things that we had never discussed. After reading Remembering Wholeness, I was able to take responsibility for my part in the failure of my marriage—sort of. It wasn't until I took the Energy Profiling class that I realized how much I had changed, not just my ex. I thought I stayed the same, allowing me to remain a victim of what had happened. He married a TYPE 2^{SM} [woman] and I changed to a TYPE 3^{SM} [woman]. I had become controlling, independent, and unforgiving.

"After my divorce I remarried. I was still struggling with not being comfortable with me, but I kept attracting people to me. Nobody seemed to know that I wasn't who I portrayed myself to be, least of all me. I was no longer taking Xanax or the antidepressants the doctors prescribed for me, but my life was still filled with anxiety. Then I started a wonderful journey when a friend loaned me Remembering Wholeness. This eventually led me to the Energy Profiling system. It was freeing to find out who I truly am. In the last couple of months, I have allowed myself to live my life as a TYPE 2^{SM} [woman] and I am finding great joy in it. The anxiety is gone because I know now that as a 2, I like to plan things out, not feeling the need to make snap decisions that I would later worry about, wondering if I made the right choices.

"I can tell my husband (he's a TYPE 1ˢᴹ [man]) that I need to take some time to wrap my brain around ideas that he has. I do give him a time limit, so he will know when he can expect an answer from me. It is good to know that when I do have to make snap decisions, my 3 energy is right there ready to step in, but no longer controls me. I can take my time and do things when I feel good about it. I am the most feminine I have ever been and am enjoying it. My husband is enjoying this softer side to me and helping me become my real self. People have noticed that I am softer, which is now a compliment to me and not a criticism.

"My husband and I have our own company. He is the TYPE 1ˢᴹ [Energy] with the ideas, and I am the TYPE 2ˢᴹ [Energy] that plans everything out.. Both of us have TYPE 3ˢᴹ Energy as our secondary which creates the action to carry through our business. Sometimes it is hard for my husband to give me the time to plan as he wants to jump right into doing, but after taking the Energy Profiling class, it makes it easier for both of us to understand why and how we can deal with things the way we do. On another note, finding out my daughter is a TYPE 4ˢᴹ [Energy] helped me understand her in a way that I never thought I could. I read book after book, trying to find ways to motivate my daughter and never making headway. Finding out she expresses a TYPE 4ˢᴹ [Energy], and that she has to be her own authority to be self motivated, has been an eye opener. When she says she doesn't care, it is nice to know that it is not a front for hidden feelings, but her actual feelings."

—PENNI ORCHARD (TYPE 2ˢᴹ ENERGY), OREGON

SUMMARY OF THE DOMINANT TYPE 2^{SM} PERSON – FLUID, FLOWING ENERGY

Oxygen/water is TYPE 2^{SM} Energy. You have an energy that is fluid and flowing. You are detail-oriented, easy-going, and are sensitive, go-with-the-flow types. TYPE 2^{SM} Energy's dominant shape in physical features is a soft flowing S curve, an oval, and a softness that is visible in their eyes, the cheeks, and the overall facial shape.

As a person who expresses TYPE 2^{SM} Energy, you may have a tendency towards these strengths:

- You have a gift of steadiness. Your strength is the steadiness and consistency you offer to others.

- You are gentle and create a soft, comfortable, safe environment.

- You are methodical in your work and absorb all the details that others may not see.

- You are kind-hearted and patient, allowing for life to flow at its pace.

- You are a connector. Connecting people, ideas, places, businesses, and happenings.

- You are subtle and your strength is in the quiet deter-mination you bring to everything.

- You are detailed, conscientious, and methodical.

- You are a peacemaker: gentle, soft, kind, sweet.

- You can see another's point of view and understand where they are coming from.

- You can accomplish many things in a calm, quiet, subtle way that is unobtrusive.

As a TYPE 2^{SM} you may have a tendency towards these challenges:

- You may get caught up in all the details and find it difficult to make decisions.

- You may be too attached to people, things, or memories and not be willing to let go so you can move forward in life.

- You may appear to be too soft, too nice, and not be able to stand your ground and share your truth or feelings.

- You may become so concerned about others' feelings that you don't acknowledge your own or give yourself value.

- You may require others to slow down because you think they need to move in a slower pattern and give more attention to details before moving forward.

TYPE 2^{SM} WORD PORTRAIT

Amenable	Comfortable	Discreet
Accommodating	Compassionate	Dreamy
Accurate	Composed	Dry humor
Agreeable	Concerned	Elegant
Appropriate	Conscientious	Eloquent
Attentive	Considerate	Empathetic
Benevolent	Consistent	Ethereal
Big hearted	Contemplative	Exquisite
Blended	Courteous	Faithful
Calm	Courtly	Fine
Careful	Delicate	Finesse
Caressing	Demure	Flowing
Cautious	Dependable	Fluid
Classical	Detailed	Fragile
Clean	Diplomatic	Gentility

Gentleness
 Good-natured
 Graceful
 Gracious
 Harmonized
 Heavenly
 Humble
 In control
 Innocent
 Insightful
 Intimate
 Intricate
 Intuitive
 Inviting
 Iridescent
 Kind
 Lavish
 Lenient
 Light touch
 Loved
 Lovely
 Loving
 Loyal
 Luscious
 Luxurious
 Meditative
 Methodical
 Meticulous
 Mist-like
 Modest
 Muted

Mysterious
Neat
Nice
Nurturing
Orderly
Organized
Particular
Patient
Peaceful
Penetrating
Persistent
Picturesque
Placid
Pleasing
Pliant
Poised
Polite
Pondering
Proper
Prudent
Quaint
Queenly
Quiet
Receptive
Relaxed
Reserved
Restful
Retiring
Romantic
Scholarly
Self-contained

Sensitive
Serene
Simple
Sincere
Soft
Softness
Soft-spoken
Soothing
Steady
Suave
Subtle
Sumptuous
Sweet
Tactful
Tender
Thoughtful
Tongue-in-cheek
Tranquil
Trustworthy
Understanding
Unflappable
Warmness
Wise
Wry

THE DOMINANT TYPE 3^{SM} PERSON

Primary Movement: *Active, Reactive*
Natural Gift: *Action*
"Let's get to work and get it done!"
Dominant Quality: *Swiftly moving us forward to our desired outcomes*

TYPE 3^{SM} ENERGY IS HYDROGEN/FIRE. Its natural primary move-ment is active and reactive. If you have a dominant TYPE 3^{SM} movement, you have an active/reactive energy. You are dynamic, sure, and purposeful. Your dominant shapes in your physical features are angles, triangles, and rectangles, which are visible in the eyes, the nose, the cheek, the hairline, and your overall body and facial shape.

TYPE 3^{SM} Energy is an extrovert expression, pushing forward with intensity to create in this world. As a person who expresses TYPE 3^{SM} Energy, you have a medium to medium-high level of movement expressing in you. This naturally dynamic, deliberate, and purposeful movement can be consistently observed through aspects of your human experience.

Other key words that describe the movement of this energy in a dominant TYPE 3^{SM} person are swift, substantial, rich, textured, intense, practical, resourceful, to-the-point, fiery, abrupt.

Due to your medium to medium-high movement that expresses itself deliberately, you may have been told a lot as a child—and even in your adult life—"Relax!" or "You're too bossy" or "Pipe down! You're too loud."

Your energy is a double yang. Your swift decisive movement is yang. Your energy pushes forward in a deliberate manner to create, which is also yang.

Your energy is like the dynamic push of Niagara Falls or the substantial depth and texture of the Grand Canyon, leaving a lasting impression with the results you create. You truly are a "ball of fire" like the great fireball the sun, just like your dominant Energy Type hydrogen/fire!

Taking action to get a result is a primary motive for a TYPE 3^{SM} person. Results are a priority in how you approach life. Action that creates results and change are important to you. Your energy is active/ reactive in its nature, which means your motive in your actions is to create a result that sets an impression that remains a long time, just like the action of the Colorado River carving a lasting impression we call the Grand Canyon! Ironically, you are not innately motivated to do what you do to impress another person; impressing others is just an outcome that naturally happens due to your dynamic energy.

When I was 15 years old, I had an experience that would have been very useful to help me better understand myself if an Energy Profiling system had existed at the time. I had long hair below my shoulders and one day I abruptly decided I wanted to get it cut. I had been given a coupon for a free haircut at the local beauty school. Since I couldn't drive and my mom and dad were out of town, I left school early, walked home (which was about three miles away), jumped on my bike and rode it 10 miles across town to the beauty school. I didn't have an appointment but they did take walk-ins. I got my haircut in a completely new style, cutting a lot of my hair off. I rode my bike home and just "got it done"! I think of that now and that screams TYPE 3^{SM} Energy all over the place. Just get it done! There are so many great clues all through our lives that point to who we truly are.

When you have your mind set on your results, your inner mantra is "to do whatever it takes" and you are willing to roll up your sleeves, get to work, and just get things done.

When I started my business over 17 years ago, I wore all the hats. I had to rely on all four of my Energy Types to launch my business—the ideas, the details, the action, and the refining. What kept me motivated was the result I had my sights set on. Even though I played all the parts, I definitely led with my TYPE 3^{SM} Energy through the experience.

I was willing to burn the candle at both ends since my actions were driven by desire to create my results. At the same time I started building my business, I had young children and I would not compromise my standards on being a good mother. This looked like a lot of late nights and early mornings to do whatever it required to achieve the results I was determined to create. I did not think much of it. In my mind, it was just what I had to do. It would bother me to be labeled a driven person or to be seen as too big a thinker. I did not understand why I did not relate to most of the women in my neighborhood who seemed so satisfied with being full-time moms. I have always had some entrepreneurial venture going on and now I understand that it was my natural ability to think big and go f or it!

I have also come to realize that people who express TYPE 3^{SM} Energy have the capacity to "burn ourselves out" more quickly than any other Energy Type, due to our swift, determined movement, which is fueled by our pronounced, substantial energy output. I have gotten into more things with great passion, gone big fast, and then grown bored and moved on to my next big life experience. For example, I started running marathons in 2001. I went on to run 16 marathons in the next four years. One day in November 2005, I just decided I was done, like Forrest in the movie Forrest Gump. He ran and ran and ran, and then just out of nowhere, he stopped and felt complete with the experience. That is very TYPE 3^{SM} movement! I created a lasting impression with all my marathon T-shirts and medals. It seems to be impressive to people, yet impressing people was never my motive in going for the results I did. I did it because I have come to learn it is my TYPE 3^{SM} nature that likes to experience life big and swift!

TYPE 3^{SM} Energy and TYPE 4^{SM} Energy are the most yang of the 4 Energy Types. What this means is they are dynamic, bold energy expressions. They have not been considered feminine in their nature in our culture of the past. Some women can confuse whether they express a dominant TYPE 3^{SM} or 4^{SM} Energy since both expressions are very strong.

Debbie felt this conflict and shares her story.

"I identified myself as a TYPE 4^{SM} [woman] at the Energy Profiling training. When the Experts explained to me that I was actually a 3 with a strong secondary 4, I disagreed. It took me a few days, but the more I thought about and considered it, the more sense it made.

"I had always thought I should be the type of person that [TYPE 4 people] are. A good person would be a 4. (I had never heard of the Energy Types but thought of the characteristics in TYPE 4^{SM} category as being ideal.) There is a lot of TYPE 4^{SM} [Energy] in me and sometimes being a 4 is what feels natural, but most of the time I tried to force myself to be 4 when I was actually feeling like I expressed TYPE 3^{SM} [Energy]. The best way to describe me was stiff, because I was being so careful to be what I was supposed to be.

"The most amazing and miraculous thing this information did for me was to help me realize that whatever I am is good—better than just good—I am wonderful just naturally as I am. I don't have to

force myself to be any particular way. I already am what I am and can just relax into it. I'm really not expected to be something else.

"Now when I notice myself thinking I should or ought to, I use it as a clue that I'm moving in the wrong direction and that I can trust myself to be what I am—which is right! It feels good."

—DEBBIE HANSEN (TYPE 3^{SM} ENERGY), COLORADO

NATURAL GIFTS AND TALENTS

In the cycle of wholeness, we have noted that the TYPE 1^{SM} Energy initiates the cycle with an idea, the TYPE 2^{SM} Energy gathers the details by asking questions and making a plan, and the TYPE 3^{SM} moves us into action. Your energy moves into action swiftly to make things happen to create a result. If you put your natural gift into a phrase, your phrase would be "Let's get to work and get it done!" As much as people with TYPE 1^{SM} Energy love starting new things, people with TYPE 3^{SM} Energy love finishing things they start. You actually only start something that you are motivated to finish, so you can experience the result of your actions. And you don't just start one thing. You have the capacity to push several things along at a time and make sure they all get done.

My daughter-in-law Sarah (TYPE 3^{SM} Energy) and I started to compare notes when she joined the family a few years ago. One thing Sarah and I both noted was how we get multiple tasks moving forward at the same time so we can get a lot of things done at once. A typical morning would look like this: taking a shower, starting to get dressed, abruptly stopping to make the bed, moving to the kitchen to start loading the dishwasher, back to the dressing, abruptly moving again to the bed, kitchen, dressing—keeping a lot of plates spinning until all the tasks are finished. If I traced my movement, it would create a lot of intersecting lines making geometric shapes, fast angles, and compartments—exactly the movement I doodle in, dress in, and express my natural self in!

My son Chris (TYPE 2^{SM} Energy) and Sarah (TYPE 3^{SM} Energy) were dating around the time I was developing the Energy Profiling information. At the time, I could not tell Sarah's dominant Energy Type. She is very blended in her movement and facial features and it was quite a mystery to me.

We had not introduced this information to her, and it has always been my rule of thumb to not tell people their Energy Type. I began to notice her tendencies as she spent more time in our home. One incident really stood out to me. Chris and Sarah came in early from a date and were talking about what to do next. I heard Sarah say to Chris, "Please, let's just clean out the car so I can check it off my list for the day!" Chris replied "It can wait, let's just relax and take it easy for a while, we've been going all day long."

Sarah, true to her TYPE 3^{SM} Energy, was interested in completing the tasks on her list to get the results she had her mind set on. Chris, true to his TYPE 2^{SM} Energy, preferred to relax and to bring comfort to their evening.

Sarah and I joke that we will write on our to-do lists tasks we have already accomplished just for the satisfaction of checking them off the list!

We also noticed one Christmas how we both have a tendency to sit back and gaze at our Christmas trees after we had finished decorating them. We realized that it is common for people with TYPE 3^{SM} Energy to gain so much pleasure in creating a result that we set aside time to take it in and bask in the pleasure of just looking at the result we accomplished!

Since I do not have any of my own TYPE 3^{SM} children, my only reference within my family had been myself for many years. I have enjoyed the insight brought by Sarah joining our family. I am also excited about my son-in-law, Tanner (TYPE 3^{SM} Energy), who recently joined the family. It's been great to have such personal interaction with a TYPE 3^{SM} male.

I believe our innate movement expresses in us from the day we are born. Tanner (TYPE 3^{SM} Energy) shared that, when he was about four years old, he had a pair of shoes that were a tiger print. He loved those shoes and wore them everyday, even to church. In fact, he has kept them all these years (you have to really love something to keep it that long, as people with TYPE 3^{SM} Energy are known to move it along and get rid of things if they do not have any practical resourceful value to them!). On the sole of the shoes was the imprint of a tiger paw. When he walked in the snow or the dirt, the shoes left a tiger paw impression. He thought it was so cool for people to think that a tiger had just come by.

If you express dominant TYPE 3^{SM} Energy, you move through life like a tiger, a very stable and deliberate movement. You jump in and take action quickly. You see what needs to be done and often wonder why no one else is jumping in to take action, assuming the rest of the world moves in your expression. You can push a lot of things forward at once, moving yourself and other people into action. You are the ready-fire-aim person, and sometimes that can burn you and others. Your primary movement is swift, intersecting, connected lines that create compartments. Rather than having one point A to point B track that you are moving on, you have at least three or more that you move things forward on. This movement would create a textured surface, which is a physical feature in TYPE 3^{SM} skin.

You can change focus abruptly, but you always come back to what you started. You are very aware of what has gone unfinished. Noticing something else can spur you into action and causes an abrupt change of focus.

My daughter Anne (TYPE 2^{SM} Energy) came over to visit last night with her husband Tanner (TYPE 3^{SM} Energy). While they were driving up the street, Tanner shared how much he loved and appreciated Anne. When he parked the car, he put his arm around her and appeared to look like he might spend some time expressing his sentiments. Then right after he shared with Anne how much he loved her, he abruptly changed focus, jumped out of the car, grabbed our snow blower, and started blowing the snow off our driveway!

Important: It is important that you acknowledge and allow your energy to have a swift, pushing nature. If you try to soften your movement and override it with apologies, it can be like a burning furnace that has no vent and will suddenly go into reactive mode— what we call rage! When you do not allow your dominant Energy Type to lead in your expressive self, you lose your connection with who you are. You will be out of balance from your active/reactive energy if you try to soften and sedate yourself.

The same natural tendencies that are your gift and talents can also be a challenge in your life, causing imbalance and disharmony. While you lead with your dominant energy, if your dominant movement takes over your life and is not balanced with the other three Energy Types (which are also a part of your being), it can be a challenge being you!

Challenge: An impediment for a TYPE 3^{SM} can be your yearning for great things with imprudent haste. You can become immediately absorbed by the aim you have in mind and rush for your goal with great haste and impetuosity. You consider too little whether you can really reach your goal because you are so sure of yourself.

Challenge: You like to create a reaction from your actions. If you are not consciously allowing your substantial energy to be expressed in a healthy way, you may subconsciously create scenarios where you say and do things just to get a reaction out of people, and most of the time it appears to be contentious! Growing up, I had no reference to what a TYPE 3^{SM} woman was like. I was exposed to a lot of TYPE

3^{SM} and 4 men, since my dad and brothers express a lot of this energy. My mom, being a TYPE 2^{SM} woman, was not a reference for me. The church I attended appeared to craft the image of the ideal woman and mom to be either a TYPE 1^{SM} or 2^{SM} expression. Not having any conscious knowledge of my inner nature, I was not able to manage it consciously to add quality to my life. It now makes sense to me why I was the catalyst to so many arguments with my TYPE 2^{SM} husband. I just wanted to experience my active/reactive nature.

My daughter Anne (TYPE 2^{SM} Energy) shared with me this story about her husband's little 5-year-old, TYPE 3^{SM} nephew. They attended a family party, and after dinner they were playing games and having fun. When the mood changed to be more sedate, the little boy kept going around the room pushing people. His mother kept telling him to stop pushing and to settle down. Anne, knowing his natural movement, started to gently push him back, creating a pushing game with him. That seemed to satisfy his need to express himself that way, and he calmed down after a few minutes of interaction.

"I had been one of the many women who felt less than beautiful. I wanted a cute little nose and thought that a nose job would do it, but would probably never do it. I saw many flaws in myself. Then I would feel guilty for those feelings. It didn't consume me or anything. I guess I just told myself my appearance was as good as it was going to get, and that I should work on being the best me.

"When I went through my transformation, a miracle occurred. My edgy haircut actually made my nose seem just right for my face. The perceived flaws were gone. I understood why I had certain features and how to make them just that—features. They are beautiful features, part of my nature, made just for me.

"... I found myself again, a happy person who finally saw the beauty inside and out. I felt like I was starting to see myself as God sees me. It was too good of a feeling to justly describe...

"My whole family dresses their truth—ages 9 to 19, and 41 and 43. We get along better and we were very close knit to begin with. We understand and enjoy one another more. We realize we don't watch TV anymore. Yes, we are busy doing good things, but when we aren't—we just sit and visit and laugh. What more could I want?

"Thank you, Carol, for this wonderful gift! Words are hard to find to truly express the way this has blessed me and my family. I wish all teenage girls knew what mine do! We are enjoying spreading the word!"

– SHEILA HANSEN (TYPE 3ˢᴹ ENERGY), WASHINGTON

PERSONALITY TRAITS

Action that creates results and lasting change or impressions are important to you. You measure results and base your success on whether or not the measured results are congruent with projected results. You can act before all the details are in place, often feeling like so many details are unnecessary as you have a deep sense of confidence and sureness about achieving success. You are very expressive about which results have been or will be achieved in your life. You can change directions abruptly and can handle diverse situations and many goals at once.

You move other people into action easily. If someone is feeling down, you will think of something to do to help the person change focus or what you can do to help fix it. You move forward with intense determination.

The dominant element that expressse in you is hydrogen/fire. Phrases commonly used to describe your personality are: "You are dynamic," or when it becomes a judgment, "You are too pushy and intense."

The two personal trainers on the hit TV show *The Biggest Loser* are both dominant TYPE 3^{SM} Energies. Both Jillian Michaels and Bob Harper are passionate about helping people get massive results in losing weight. If you want to see TYPE 3^{SM} Energy at its best, watch this show. They have a fiery push in getting people to work harder than they have ever worked in their life to reach their dreams. They are not acting. It is their active/reactive energy coming through. To help someone lose over 150 pounds in a few months takes TYPE 3^{SM} Energy!

> **Challenge:** You can burn out by getting too much going on, making too many commitments, and taking action too soon.

TYPE 3^{SM} Energy is very passionate. Whenever you are bent on carrying out your plans, or find opposition, you are filled with passionate excitement. You can become addicted to action! If someone challenges you or suggests you can't do what you are desiring, you most likely are thinking, "Oh yeah, just watch me!" You are very self-confident and self-reliant and tend to take success for granted because you expect it.

You have the most competitive nature of all the Energy Types, with the TYPE 4^{SM} Energy close behind you. You are just as competitive with yourself as you are as an opponent. Tanner (TYPE 3^{SM} Energy) and I were playing tennis on a recent vacation. Tanner won the match just slightly. After the match, Anne (TYPE 2^{SM} Energy) asked us both if, when we lose a game, do we then go over it in our minds to see what we could have done better or what we could have done differently to win? Tanner and I just looked at each other and I replied, "No, that is too much detail. I just figure I should have won and I just want to play again so I can." All while Tanner nodded in agreement with me.

Challenge: You can be impetuous and impulsive in a big way, plunging into situations where forethought would have benefited you.

THOUGHT AND FEELING PROCESSES

Your thoughts and feelings are swift and deliberate. You compartmentalize your thoughts to keep track of all the activities you have put into motion. You compartmentalize things in your head and can move from one compartment to the next easily, without losing concentration because it all has a purpose to you.

You do not like to take time to read instructions in detail as you have confidence that you will be able to figure it out as you go. You think first about the result and outcome to be achieved than what it will take to get there. You like to move into action quickly.

Communication: You value honest communication, credibility, and realism. You like to get to the point in your communication. In fact, a common phrase you will use when someone is dragging things out is, "What's your point?" Going over too many details can bog you down. You are good at delegating. When you feel someone is credible and they get results, you give them free reign to do what has been delegated to them. You don't like to beat around the bush, and you are practical and honest in your communications.

You value your accomplishments, the results you create in life. You like talking about your results and accomplishments readily. It may appear to others that you are bragging, but results are such a central focus of your movement that you don't think of it as bragging. Since you are not motivated by impressing people, it surprises you when people think of you this way.

Detailed journal keeping is not usually of value to you. If you do keep a journal, it is probably done more in a style of bullet points.

116

My daughter Anne (TYPE 2^{SM} Energy) shared the following about her husband Tanner (TYPE 3^{SM} Energy), "After looking at my many detailed journals from age 8 and up, Tanner told me that I could read over his journals in about 20 minutes. Some of his journal entries from fifth grade include: "I'm the best quarterback in the 5th grade," and "I made three touchdowns today! I'm the best quarterback in the 5th grade."

"Before discovering the Energy Profiling system, I always focused on what was wrong with me. Growing up, I tried to be like my big sister. She was the beauty queen, the star soprano in chorus, the favorite babysitter of all the neighbors. She was even valedictorian of our high school.

"We looked totally different, too. She had the skin that would tan, the small waist and the very feminine hands. I got the freckles and red hair, the boyish figure, and more masculine hands. My face was also more angular with a high forehead. I was always trying to hide my so-called flaws.

"I used to feel almost apologetic for being competitive and driven. I thought I was that way, in part, because I was always trying to match up to my big sister. Even my friends would tell me I work too hard, and to sit back and smell the roses.

"I currently have two businesses, and I love them both. But I've always felt I had to make excuses for being so driven. The truth is, I can't stand sitting around doing nothing. Again, I thought I just have some psychological hang up.

"Then I discovered I'm a TYPE 3^{SM} Energy Type. And TYPE 3^{SM} [Energy] loves action! They also do well in business and make good leaders. And even their physical characteristics are more yang or what I used to call masculine. I finally felt it's okay to be me, just the way I am!

"I no longer compare myself to others, thinking I should be more like them. In fact, I can now figure out their Energy Type, and know why they respond the way they do. It all makes such perfect sense now. For instance, my husband is a TYPE 4^{SM} [man]. He is so black-and-white about things, he should have been a policeman! I, on the other hand, being a TYPE 3^{SM} [Energy], feel like rules are made to be broken. When I'm driving, I'm going to push the speed limit as much as I can (as a TYPE 3^{SM} [person] I like to go fast). My husband, on the other hand, will purposefully drive five miles under the speed limit, which I find excruciatingly s-l-o-w! But I see how we balance each other out. My strengths and his strengths complement each other.

"My friends have noticed that I assert myself more now. Where before I would go along with whatever restaurant or movie just to please them, now I state what I really want. I feel so much happier now. No more feeling like I have to hide myself or my true feelings."

—KAY SMITH (TYPE 3^{SM} ENERGY), TEXAS

BEHAVIOR TENDENCIES

Your behavior tendencies express like a hawk, moving along deliberately with your eye on the result you want, spotting opportunities, and moving swiftly into action to create it.

Relationships: You are open in your relationships, eager to work things out with your loved ones. You express a great deal of love and affection for the select people you form deeper relationships with.

Social: You have the confidence to interact with anyone. You are friendly and talkative in social situations. You have no problem starting a conversation in the grocery store checkout line.

Timeliness: You may have a tendency for being late due to your tendency to want to get so much done. You are not realistic about what can really been finished in the time allotted and will try and do it anyway. Being late sets the stage for you to move into swift action, getting done what you want before you leave for your destination.

Work: You are reliable. You excel in positions that allow you to take the lead, motivate others, and challenge your entrepreneurial spirit. It is common for a person with TYPE 3^{SM} Energy to pursue an entrepreneurial opportunity in their professional career. People who dominantly express TYPE 3^{SM} Energy are not afraid of doing their own thing due to their high level of confidence. Your reputation is, "You can count on them to get the job done."

Challenge: You tend to dominate people of other Energy Types in work settings, especially TYPE 2^{SM} co-workers.

Money: You are good with money and have a strong focus on it. Money is a measurement of your results in your professional activities. The more money you are making, the more you are getting the results you want with your profession or business pursuits.

Physical Activity: You prefer group activities and competition. You love to challenge yourself and win. You are a very physical person, enjoying everything from exercise or adventure trips to wrestling with your kids. It is common for a you to love sports, whether you are watching them or participating in them. Years ago I got bored with my daily exercise routine. That is when I started to train for marathons. I found that, with my TYPE 3^{SM} Energy, I was more motivated to get up early and train for an event that I wanted to be prepared for, rather than just exercise without the bigger goal. Since I have given up marathon running, I switched to competing in sprint-distance triathlons. Last year, I had a goal to compete in one triathlon a month from April through November. I successfully met my goal and had a lot of fun doing it. Ironically, I have noticed that most of the people competing in triathlons are TYPE 3^{SM} athletes, especially in the women's divisions.

BODY LANGUAGE

You may or may not have a predominant amount of TYPE 3^{SM} Energy expressing through your body language and physical features. Most people are blended in their physical features, so you won't see yourself in all these expressions, but you will notice many expressions of TYPE 3^{SM} body language and physical features if you are a dominant TYPE 3^{SM} person.

Walking: You walk with a determination in your step, with a firm plant of your feet, quick and brisk. Everyone can hear you coming.

Sitting/Standing: People can even hear you sit, due to your deliberate movement. You create angles when you sit and stand. Legs crossed, one leg pulled up under you, head cocked to the side, hands on waist, or your body bent at the waist.

Voice /Language: A TYPE 3^{SM} voice is brassy with a medium to low pitch. You can speak explosively in volume at times. Your language can be intense, reactive, abrupt, and sassy.

Doodling: You doodle using shapes that represent your natural movement, that is, angles, geometric shapes in all directions. For an example of TYPE 3^{SM} doodles, see www.myenergyprofile. com/doodle.

Personal Space: You know where everything is because you compartmentalize things in your mind. You can have a lot out and around, but can get it cleaned up swiftly. You don't mind cleaning up after yourself because the mess enabled you to experience the result of the effort expended. Due to your practical nature, what you own needs to be useful to you. You may be known for getting rid of things too quickly or throwing away your children's homework.

Interior Design: You prefer your surroundings to be casual, natural, and rich in color and texture.

"When I found out I was a TYPE 3ᔆᴹ [Energy], I had several huge reactions. First, absolute shock and disbelief. Disbelief, because I couldn't believe that I was so powerful and amazing. I had definitely not been living the truth of who I was, and my mother had unknowingly tried to quiet me down as a child and make me more ladylike. It all makes sense now as my [TYPE 2ᔆᴹ] mother... just thought I should be more like her. She didn't understand how very different I am.

"The other huge reaction I had was this tremendous emotional release. I cried off and on for several days. I had never felt more validated. I was so relieved that I didn't have to be somebody else anymore. It was just okay to be me. It was like I was releasing this artificial shell that had been with me for years. I spent a lot of time alone just processing and shifting internally.

"What followed next has been the most beautiful journey of self-love. I began to love and cherish myself more and more. It's so much more fun to be me now, and I just laugh at myself at times. I no longer make myself wrong for not being more girlish or detailed or whatever it is that I'm just not. It's just okay now. And as I love and accept myself more, I find myself able to love and accept the people around me much more as well."

—KIMBERLEE SUMMURS (TYPE 3ᔆᴹ ENERGY), CALIFORNIA

"I thought I was failing at being a wife, mother, and friend. I was forcing life. I saw my accomplishments as very little when compared to others. Learning my Energy Type helped me see, not just how, but why I moved the way I did. I quickly let go of trying to be someone I was not. I then shifted to celebrating who I am. I think knowing how my thoughts are processed has been the biggest help to me. I know my natural abilities and tendencies, and that alone is powerful information. I have a clear direction for my life now and live my life as the dynamic and inspiring woman I was created to be!"

—KRISTA NEBEKER (TYPE 3ᔆᴹ ENERGY), IDAHO

PHYSICAL FEATURES

The overall quality of your physical expression is earthy, textured, natural, and exotic. Your bone structure has angles and is chiseled, giving a look of strength with your features being asymmetrical.

Skin and Skin Texture: TYPE 3ᔆᴹ skin has an irregular pigment, sunspots, age spots, rough, textured, deeper lines, and can be prone to acne. If you have TYPE 3ᔆᴹ skin, you may have been investing time and money trying to eliminate the natural features of your 3-ness expressing in your skin. I have TYPE 3ᔆᴹ skin and I have learned that it is best to work with this expression rather than against it. By not trying to make my skin be something it is not, I support bringing out the natural beauty of my skin rather than trying to change it.

When I am dressing my truth and have a hairstyle in the right color, cut and style, I enhance the appearance of my skin by having the right movement and vibration around my face. The result is that the features in my skin that I once saw as flaws, I now experience as naturally beautiful and I feel grateful for them. I am also grateful to share this information, especially with TYPE 3^{SM} men and women who may be investing in anti-aging products with little result. I have come up with the best anti-aging system for every Energy Type, but especially for someone who expresses TYPE 3^{SM} Energy: it is the right haircut for your Energy Type!

Face Shape: Triangular, angular facial planes, square or angular jaw, chiseled edges.

Cheeks: Various forms of triangles on cheeks, and/or around mouth.

Nose: Angular, beak, knobby, lump of clay, with triangular nostrils.

Eyebrows: Come to a peak somewhere after the middle of the eye.

Eyes: Come to a point in the inside of the eyes or outside corners, angles above the eyes in the lid area to create a very exotic look.

Hands: Rough, textured, knobby knuckles, spots, veiny, lots of pigmentation. It is common for someone with TYPE 3^{SM} hands to comment that they think their hands look old due to these features.

FAMOUS PEOPLE

Women: Raquel Welch, Tina Turner, Katharine Hepburn, Barbara Walters, Michelle Obama, Whoopi Goldberg, Susan Sarandon, Beyonce Knowles, Oprah Winfrey, Maria Shriver, Stockard Channing, Rosa Parks, Amelia Earhart

Men: Barack Obama, Viggo Mortensen, Arnold Schwarzenegger, Brad Pitt, Paul Newman, Richard Branson, Conan O'Brian, Michael Phelps, Daniel Craig, Lance Armstrong, John Madden, Hugh Jackman, Jackie Robinson

MUSIC AND MUSICIANS

Music that has high movement, is brash, active, and dynamic is TYPE 3^{SM} music. A notable example is "William Tell Overture" by Gioachino Rossini. A few TYPE 3^{SM} musicians include Phil Collins, Rod Stewart, Ray Charles, David Cook, Rolling Stones, Avril Lavigne, Creedence Clearwater Revival, Tom Petty, U2, Alanis Morrisette, and Journey.

NATIONS

The United States and Russia competed for years to see who could be the biggest, the best and the most dominant presence on the planet.

HOW YOUR ENERGY AFFECTS OTHER PEOPLE

Your energy leaves an impression, which makes you noticed by others. You get people moving into action. Your active/reactive energy moves people into action. You are naturally a leader to others. You may notice that family and friends turn to you to take the lead, to make decisions and lead out. For example, on a family vacation, you may be the one who decides which activities to do each day and gets everybody moving in that direction. When we went out to dinner one night with a large number of our family members, my daughter-in-law Sarah (TYPE 3^{SM} Energy), who was very new to the family, noticed the need to decide what flavor and sizes of pizzas to order. She naturally took charge of getting the group to make the decision and called the waitress over to place the order. At times, others can experience your energy as overbearing, pushy, and insensitive. You can be judged as being too much to handle and overconfident.

FOR OTHERS: CREATING A SUCCESSFUL RELATIONSHIP WITH A DOMINANT TYPE 3^{SM} PERSON

DOs

Honor their active/reactive, determined nature by letting them take the lead when appropriate. Praise their ability to make decisions quickly and don't tell them they can't do it. Rather, join in with their confidence and engage them in a conversation about any considerations you are noticing that would be helpful to them to take note of and plan for before they jump right in.

Know that their true nature—the natural movement expressing through them—is swift, substantial, dynamic, abrupt, and to the point. As you accept that, you accept them.

DON'Ts

Don't tell a TYPE 3^{SM} person to relax or take it easy when they are getting worked up about something. That is like telling Niagara Falls to stop flowing! Rather support them by saying, "Wow, you're getting fired up about that. It's important to you, isn't it?"

Don't set yourself up to be disappointed by placing your expectations of how you (in your Energy Type) would move through life, and what you would do to get from point A to point B. It will not look the same to a TYPE 3^{SM} person. TYPE 3^{SM} people move very swiftly, determined to finish what they set out to do.

Jonathan and I had just returned home from an evening out. Since we work together in our own business, we have a great opportunity to experience each other a lot. A typical pattern we can find ourselves in is our very different approach (movement) to how we do business. In my 3-ness, I like to get things done swiftly. I like moving things forward quickly and I operate with a lot of confidence that it will all work out. I have a ready-fire-aim approach to moving forward.

Jonathan expresses a dominant TYPE 2^{SM} Energy and is more methodical and thinks things through. He asks a lot more questions than I do. He gathers information and deliberates longer when I like to just get going.

During our evening out, we had discussed some business topics. I was feeling frustrated and bothered that some things were taking so long to get done. I was expressing my frustration in what appeared to be a more intense manner than my husband would ever express himself. In the middle of my venting, he said to me, "Relax, it is going to be okay, just take it easy." At that moment I had an Energy Profiling lightning bolt moment, a moment where I was opened to more understanding to what supports us and what shuts us down to our true selves.

I realized that telling someone of a dominant TYPE 3^{SM} Energy movement to "relax" and "take it easy" is not supportive. I realized that I had been told that a lot through my entire life, and attempting to do that was going completely against my nature. Try telling Niagara Falls to relax, take it easy, you are just too much power!

I started to laugh and shared my insight with Jonathan. I said, "You know, that is not what supports me right now. I would feel supported if you told me that you can see I really feel strongly about this, and encourage me to get fired up and go for it because I feel so passionately about it."

I realized that hearing that would give me support and would add permission to just be me. In allowing me to be me, balance comes into play and I naturally shift into more alignment and ease with who I am. It is when I don't feel like I can be in my natural movement and expression that I force it, and it comes out amplified and unattractive, defeating my purpose of what I am trying to accomplish.

With this realization, I was able to write what to say and not to say to each Energy Type that supports us in being our true nature. You can find these in each of the Energy Type sections under the "For Others" category.

"Through the last 28 years of life—being widowed after three months of marriage, an instant stepson, three sons of my own, a husband whom I adore that has had two stress breakdowns, and a few physical health challenges—had squashed who I am/was and never even knew it.

"Going to the Energy Profiling event started an awareness inside of me and got me so excited I felt like I was going to burst. I wanted to know more and I wanted it now... This process has been great for my soul, my family, and those around me. My hubby loves my shift and notices that I am changing... Thank you for the fun new journey."

—DIANE ADAMS (TYPE 3^{SM} ENERGY), UTAH

"Where do I begin to say thank you for improving my marriage, my relationship with nine children, and helping me to like myself? I am a TYPE 3^{SM} with a secondary 4. My family saw me as overbearing, domineering, judgmental, eccentric, cluttery, and so forth. What the Energy Profiling system has done for our family is to see each other's strengths and weaknesses, and I now can see myself through different eyes. I know I can be overwhelming to people of different... Energy Types and I try to honor that, and they in turn honor my strengths. It has helped me equally well in my business. I know better how to help them use their strengths to build their businesses. The list could go on and on. I, for one, will be eternally grateful for what I have learned. Thank you so much for developing and teaching this wonderful way to understand and appreciate the differences in each of us."

—LEIANN KING (TYPE 3^{SM} ENERGY), UTAH

SUMMARY OF THE DOMINANT TYPE 3ᴿᴹ PERSON – ACTIVE, REACTIVE ENERGY

Hydrogen/fire is TYPE 3ˢᴹ Energy. People in this category have an active/reactive energy. These people are results-oriented, passionate people. Their dominant shape in physical features is the triangle and is visible in the eyebrows, eyes, and cheeks and overall facial shape.

As a person who expresses dominant TYPE 3ˢᴹ Energy, you may have a tendency towards these strengths:

- You are a radiant source of movement and energy—a fireball.

- You are action-oriented with a driving force to accomplish or compete.

- You have an abundance of sureness about moving forward, and you inspire others to have confidence in you even if you don't feel confident.

- You have the capacity to accomplish big things in a big way. You think big.

- You are an entrepreneur by nature and can easily figure out ways to make money doing what you like to do.

- You are a natural salesperson. You know how to promote and bring in the buyer. And you also know how to close the deal.

- You are an independent soul and do not need approval from others to move forward.

- You are decisive and can easily "take the ball and run with it."

- You are task-oriented and can solve problems and get results very quickly.

- You are deliberate and to-the-point in all that you do.

As a person who expresses dominant TYPE 3^{SM} Energy, you may have a tendency toward these challenges:

- You may hold others to your high standard of accomplishment and think of them as inferior.

- You may be too pushy, too aggressive, too bossy or too abrupt for other Energy Types.

- You may be inconsiderate of other people's feelings when you're on a path to accomplish something and they get in your way.

- You may be moving forward so quickly that you don't take the time to get all the details.

- You may think that it has to fit your way of doing it or it's just nonsense.

TYPE 3^{SM} WORD PORTRAIT

Abrupt	Complex	Enterprising
Active	Confident	Entrepreneur
Adventurous	Daring	Exciting
Aggressive	Decisive	Exotic
Ambitious	Determined	Expressive
Angled	Direct	Fast
Assertive	Down to business	Fervent
Assured	Driven	Fiery
Asymmetrical	Dynamic	Forceful
Authoritative	Eager	Frank
Big-hearted	Earnest	Gallant
Business-minded	Earthy	Generous
Captivating	Edgy	Get the job done
Casual	Encouraging	High-spirited
Competitive	Energetic	Hot

Independent

Industrious

Informal

Intense

Inventive

Jagged

Lavish

Levelheaded

Logical

Loud

Lusty

Magnetic

Metallic

Mover & shaker

No frills

No fuss

Outgoing

Passionate

Persevering

Persistent

Pioneering

Powerful

Practical

Pragmatic

Profoundness

Promoter

Protective

Purposeful

Pushy

Quick

Reactive

Realistic

Resourceful

Restless

Result driven

Rich

Rough

Rowdy

Rugged

Rustic

Self-confident

Self-disciplined

Self-reliant

Self-starter

Social

Solid

Solution-oriented

Spicy

Spirited

Strong

Substantial

Sultry

Sure

Swift

Take charge

Tenacious

Textured

To the point

Unevenness

Verve

Vigorous

Vitality

Vivid

Warmth

Wild

Zesty

THE DOMINANT TYPE 4^{SM} PERSON

Primary Movement: *Constant, Still*
Natural Gift: *Perfecting*
"Here's how we can make it better!"
Dominant Quality: *Serenely reflecting truth back to us and improving the quality of our lives*

TYPE 4^{SM} ENERGY IS CARBON/EARTH. Its natural primary movement is constant and still. If you have a dominant TYPE 4^{SM} movement, you have a constant, still energy. You are reflective, concise, and clear. The dominant shapes in your physical features are elongated ovals with straight sides, diagonal parallel lines in any direction, which are visible in the eyes, the nose, the cheek, the hairline, and overall body and facial shape.

TYPE 4^{SM} Energy is a reflective, still expression with a quality that mirrors exactness and balance back to us. You have the lowest level of natural inner movement of all the Energy Types. This natural, keen, precise, still movement can be consistently observed through many aspects of your human experience.

Other key words that describe the movement of this energy in a dominant TYPE 4^{SM} person are: bold, authoritative, keen, regal, polished, striking, sleek, structured, clean, clear, simple, reflective, exact, and grounding.

Due to your low to no movement that expresses itself as solid and structured, you may have been told a lot as a child, and even in your adult life, to "Lighten up!" or "Don't be so critical or serious."

Your energy is both yin and yang. Your stillness and reflective quality is your yin movement, and your energy creates structure, which is your yang movement.

Your energy has the firm and statuesque presence of a noble fir tree or the reflective quality of a still lake mirroring perfection back to the world.

Keeping things structured and staying on track is the primary motive for a TYPE 4ˢᴹ person. Creating quality and precision is a priority in how you approach life. The movement of TYPE 4ˢᴹ Energy is the most rigid of all the Energy Types. For this reason I have noticed that, of all the Energy Types, TYPE 4ˢᴹ Energy is the most misunderstood and can be the most misjudged and unappreciated. We tend to perceive this energy as authoritative, critical, and more serious. Understanding this movement gives us the opportunity to understand your TYPE 4ˢᴹ nature with more respect and honor for the gift and talent you so beautifully bring to the whole.

I have the great blessing of currently having three dominant TYPE 4ˢᴹ members in our family—my son Mark, my son-in-law Tony, and my grandson Seth. I started to develop this information when my son Mark (TYPE 4ˢᴹ Energy) was about 16 years old. Understanding the dynamics of his natural, core movement and how it expresses through so many aspects of his life, has been one of the most valuable insights I could ever hope for as his mother. Being able to honor and understand his constant still nature, and what that looks like in his everyday tendencies as a person, has allowed me to see and experience his truth, and to respect and honor him deeply when I could have easily misunderstood the exact same tendencies as negative personality traits. My son-in-law, Tony (TYPE 4ˢᴹ Energy), recently told my daughter Jenny (TYPE 1ˢᴹ Energy), "I feel like your mom understands me better than any person I know." Coming from a TYPE 4^{SM} person, that is an incredible compliment and honor to be acknowledged that way.

If you express dominant TYPE 4^{SM} Energy, you do not typically look to outside sources to help you understand yourself better. One of your tendencies is to be deeply reflective, and to pride yourself in knowing who you are. I have not yet found a personality profile system that truly recognizes you, and honors who you are, and I can see why you would consider them to be a waste of your time.

A TYPE 4^{SM} person likes to play by the rules—to color within the lines—but only as long as you trust the source of the rules and the rules themselves. Once you respect and accept the authority of another person or an organization, the rules they lay down are easier for you to keep, even if you do not fully agree with those rules. More than just following rules, you also likes to create rules for others to follow.

Let me first say that I recognize you to be the authority in your own world. I offer you the Energy Profiling model as an opportunity to add to your already-clear understanding of who you are and what is important to you. I have learned that you generally don't like being told what Energy Type you are, especially if you are a TYPE 4^{SM}. I honestly don't believe we can tell anyone what Energy Type they express. No two people are exactly alike, but I think you will agree with me that even you, in your expression of TYPE 4^{SM} Energy, have some uncanny similarities that you will recognize in yourself and others as you read through this section. My hope for you is that you will allow yourself to use this information to add quality to your relationships and your life. Let me illustrate that with a comment I heard not long ago. A TYPE 4^{SM} woman shared with me, "I believe this information could have helped me turn my marriage around before we divorced."

TYPE 4^{SM} and TYPE 3^{SM} Energy are the most yang of the four Energy Types. This means that you are dynamic, bold energy expressions. The nature of these Types of women has not been considered feminine in our culture of the past. This can be especially challenging for a dominant TYPE 4^{SM} woman. I am grateful to offer this information to help everyone live their truth, no matter their gender!

"Learning my Energy Type has resulted in profound changes in my life. My profile was exactly what I thought it wasn't, and I had a hard time accepting it as I had strong judgments on myself and my way of being.

"I was living primarily in my secondary type, always wanting to be something completely different—hiding out and not feeling authentic. I could never put my finger on why. Learning my profile brought clarity to my gifts and had such a grounding effect on me. I was finally comfortable being quiet and contemplative in the company of others, finally appreciating my ability to see things with a critical eye as a gift. I have become more willing to say things directly, rather than beat around the bush to be nice out of fear of judgment.

"This shift for me has created shifts in many of my relationships—some ending, some new ones forming, some deepening—but in all of them I feel more true to myself and a deeper and better appreciation of others, especially my family. Learning my profile has been a springboard for me to new possibilities in my life—a reopening of spirit within me, you could say. I feel strong and hopeful, and blessed to have been so validated by learning this information!"

—JEAN DIXON (TYPE 4^{SM} ENERGY), ILLINOIS

NATURAL GIFTS AND TALENTS

TYPE 4^{SM} Energy completes our cycle of wholeness. For a recap, TYPE 1^{SM} Energy starts the cycle by initiating an idea with the hope it can be done, TYPE 2^{SM} Energy gathers the details to make the plan, TYPE 3^{SM} Energy pushes us into action, and TYPE 4^{SM} Energy has a keen awareness to step back and analyze the whole process and consider what has been created to see how it can be improved.

If you put your natural gift into a phrase, your phrase would be, "Here is how we can make it better, and here is how we can duplicate it." You truly see the world through a critical eye for perfecting it. Because of your reflective quality, you not only want to perfect the world, you want to share what you believe brings quality to our lives by duplicating it and sharing it.

People who express TYPE 4^{SM} Energy step back from a situation rather than jumping into it. This allows you to take in the bigger picture and see what is going on.

Your keen eye and gift of precision help you see all the pieces and how they fit together to create a perfect whole. You have the gift of being able to make anything more perfect and systemize any process to a desired, repeatable, and predictable outcome. You take things to their final perfected form.

Your primary shape is reflecting, parallel lines. You can see the straight line in your movement from point A to point B. You move through life taking the direct, straightforward route, once you have determined the exact goal. One of the dominant shapes in your facial features (such as the bridge of your nose) is parallel lines moving in any direction—horizontal, vertical, and a fast diagonal line.

You have a naturally keen view of your world, and when you feel so inspired, you share your awareness in a very concise manner. You can't help that what you first see is what is weak or at fault. You may not always share this insight, but you will always lead with those thoughts.

I am eager for my son Mark (TYPE 4^{SM} Energy) to create a career where his natural gift of perfecting the world can be channeled for everyone's benefit. I came to realize that during his youth and young adult years, when he was still in high school. Now that he is in college, I have yet another opportunity to help channel his gift of perfecting the world, to be something more of value to him. I often see and experience his tendency to critically comment on TV commercials, cars, the way people drive, and other things that don't really matter in the bigger scheme of things. Knowing his gift for perfecting things, and his tendency to see what he perceives as weakness, I don't make much of it and thank him for his awareness. In taking that approach, I honor his TYPE 4^{SM} movement and expression.

Important: It is important to your TYPE 4^{SM} nature that you acknowledge and allow your energy to have a precise and structured nature. If you try to lighten up your movement and become more random and animated, your 4-ness will bleed through and, quite honestly, that can shock people! When you do not allow your dominant Energy Type to lead in your expressive self, you lose your connection with who you are. You will be out of balance from your constant, still energy if you try to force yourself to lighten up and animate yourself. You are not able to fake how you feel. My son Mark (TYPE 4^{SM} Energy) admits that he cannot force or fake his feelings. For example, if he were given a gift for his birthday that he does not feel excited about, he can politely receive and appreciate it, but he can't fake being excited about it. It's just not available to him in his movement. In 2008, the hit Broadway play Mamma Mia became a popular movie starring Meryl Streep (TYPE 1^{SM} Energy) and Pierce Brosnan (TYPE 4^{SM} Energy). Meryl Streep, due to her naturally animated nature, shined in the movie. Pierce Brosnan, due to his naturally still nature, came off rigid and stiff in the singing and dancing scenes. Casting directors could benefit from a knowledge of the Energy Profiling system!

Another amazing gift you share with humanity through your TYPE 4^{SM} nature is your energetic gift of reflecting truth back to others. When you live in harmony with your true nature, you naturally reflect the truth of others back to them. You are an energetic mirror for others, sending the silent message, "Be true to yourself, and believe in yourself." There is nothing you have to do; just being present offers this gift.

The same natural tendencies that are your gifts and talents can also be a challenge in your life, causing temporary imbalance and disharmony. You always lead with your dominant Energy Type. But when your dominant movement takes over your life and is not balanced with the other three Energy Types (which are also a part of your being), it can be a challenge being you!

Challenge: You may appear harsh, judgmental or too opinionated. Because you have this tendency to see the weakness first, you can come across as too critical and negative. Knowing this about yourself, you can manage your gift with more awareness and choose how you express your insights in a manner that does not appear overly critical. You may have even tried to become less judgmental, less critical, and less bold, because you have been told too often that these are purely negative attributes. However, it is impossible to hide your gifts of discernment because, though you can always improve your behaviors, you cannot change your inner nature. It is your blueprint.

PERSONALITY TRAITS

You are your own authority. You do not give that authority to others, but will look to others you perceive as an authority—in their expertise in life—to guide you in your interests. If you perceive their authority as trustworthy, you will follow their guidance and rules; if you do not trust their authority, you may abide their rules for a time to get to someplace you want to go. If someone tries to be an uninvited authority over you, you think in your mind, "I didn't ask you to tell me what to do or how to do it." You would be especially sensitive to not welcoming this kind of feedback if it came from someone you viewed to be no more an authority over a topic or situation than you are.

"Coming to recognize and embrace my Energy Type has been an incredible experience, particularly considering that, [with a TYPE 4ᴿᴹ Energy], those of my type are quite reticent to embrace—let alone acknowledge—the Energy Profiling program as a legitimate and powerful method for understanding one's true nature (even more so than men generally)... I've been able to see and understand myself as the true sovereign energy I am, fully (and finally) embracing my own authority. It has been the most liberating experience of my life. Period."

—JR PETERSON (TYPE 4ˢᴹ ENERGY)

You look at what has been created with a critical eye and opinion to evaluate and determine what could be done better, faster, and more efficiently. You have a keen focus and you stay on course easily. You also demand perfection and want to make things the best they can be. Because of your TYPE 4ˢᴹ nature, you expect the best from others and hold a high standard. You move forward with crystal-clear, focused determination, with a quiet confidence that you can do it better than most people.

The dominant element expressing in you is carbon/earth. Phrases used to describe your personality are: "You are such a pillar of strength." Or when it becomes a judgment, "You take things too seriously or literally!"

You do not like being put in the limelight spontaneously; however, when you choose it, you are very effective in influencing others. For example, it was my son Mark's (TYPE 4^{SM} Energy) birthday. He came home from school that day and I asked him how his day had been. He replied, "It was the worst day of my life!" I asked him why and he shared, "I walked into the lunch room and all my friends started singing 'Happy Birthday' to me in front of everyone! I turned around and walked out because it was so uncomfortable for me."

The irony in this quality is that you are the most striking people in the world, and you can't help but stand out, especially when you dress true to your nature.

I see some of the most remarkable transformations occur when TYPE 4^{SM} women and men learn to dress true to their Energy Type. Often, they don't especially stand out before they dress their truth. But after they apply what they have learned, they are some of the most noticeable individuals I meet. They are striking and immediately stand out due to their naturally stunning appearance. You need to recognize that, even though you may not want a lot of attention drawn to you, your stunning looks naturally get the attention of others.

> **Challenge:** Your presence of authority and boldness can unknowingly feel intimidating to others. You may have been judging this quality as negative and trying to lighten or soften yourself. An easier way to deal with this quality is to realize that others are giving you unspoken authority to initiate interaction with them. You would actually prefer it this way, as you are not fond of random interactions at the whim of others. You prefer to choose who you would like to interact with and whom you invite into your personal space.

Challenge: You can get stuck by wanting every little part and piece perfect, demanding too much of yourself and others, not wanting to get off track. You need to learn to say, "It's good enough," and move on. And rather than try to perfect everything, channel your gift into what truly is important to you and adds quality to your life and those you love. Then let the rest—those things that aren't that important to you—be good enough.

Challenge: More than any other Energy Type, you will find it harder to change your direction when things are not working out, especially if they were well planned in the first place.

On a family vacation, we were all playing a DVD game. The game was a guessing game, was poorly designed, and had resourced little-known songs for the samples of tunes from which you could guess. With the mix of Energy Types we have in our family, it was interesting to see how things played out.

Within five to ten minutes of playing the game, it was a group con-sensus that the game was not much fun and in the words of the TYPE 4^{SM} family members, it was "pretty stupid!" But we still kept playing. The first two to drop out of the game were my TYPE 1^{SM} daughter Jenny and TYPE 1^{SM} son Mario, as they were the least attached and were not having fun. Then my TYPE 2^{SM} husband Jonathan and TYPE 2^{SM} daughter Anne fell asleep. I stopped playing, and wound up having more fun noticing what was happening within the group dynamics. (Actually, I knew if I observed, I would have more teaching material.) At this point, three people were still playing the game: my son Chris who has a very strong secondary TYPE 4^{SM} expression, my son Mark, and son-in-law Tony, both TYPE 4^{SM}s.

They continued to play the game, criticizing it the entire time, but still finishing what they had started. I realized from this experience that it is the most difficult for people with TYPE 4^{SM} Energy to disengage and change what they set out to do. They get on a track and stay on that track until they reach the point of completion, the point they have set in their mind to reach. As a TYPE 4^{SM}, you may even find it hard to stop reading a book that you started, even if you do not like it!

You are private, disciplined, influential, and uncompromising in your approach to life. When my son-in-law Tony (TYPE 4^{SM} Energy) was a first year medical student at The Ohio State University, he was able to choose an independent study track. This basically was like homeschooling himself the first year. He spent hours and hours each day in a study cubicle memorizing material from his textbooks, preparing to take exams. His natural ability to create structure, and within that structure be intensely focused, supported him in successfully completing his first year with flying colors.

His wife Jenny (TYPE 1^{SM} Energy) has learned that when Tony has time to relax and have fun, it suits him to have an agreed-upon starting time and finishing time for his leisure time. Within this structure, he can really let his studies go, knowing there will be a time he gets back on track with them.

> **Challenge:** Due to your gift of perfecting things in your environment, you have a tendency to set standards that neither you nor anyone else can meet. This can set you up to feel that you can never fulfill your desired expectations, and always fall short of the mark. With your tendency towards perfection, you can create low self-esteem and pessimism in your view of yourself, others, and life in general.

> **Challenge:** You steer away from things that you cannot easily be perfect in. Your tendency for high expectations can place a great demand on yourself, and you may be

limiting your interests and opportunity to try new things due to your perfecting nature.

THOUGHT AND FEELING PROCESSES

Your thoughts and feelings are deep and reflective. Your thoughts are far reaching and penetrating. You are not satisfied with the superficial. You search for the cause and correlation of things, seeking to understand the laws that effect human life and the principles by which you guide your life. You are a clear thinker and a thorough and efficient organizer of your thoughts. It is important for you to mentally organize your thoughts so you can move forward within a framework of structure. You are not at ease until this state has been achieved. You take in a lot of information and can quickly figure out what has value to you and what does not.

You tend to take things literally in black and white terms. One afternoon, I ran an errand with my daughter Anne (TYPE 2^{SM} Energy) and son-in-law Tony (TYPE 4^{SM} Energy). Anne wanted to engage Tony in some friendly chit-chat. She asked him, "Do you have any good music on your iPod, Tony?" In Tony's TYPE 4^{SM} sense of humor he replied, "No, Anne, I only have bad music on my iPod!" In Tony's mind, he would only have music he liked and judged as good on his iPod. There was no gray area.

You really have a very soft-hearted disposition. You reveal your innermost thoughts and feelings reluctantly and only to those whom you trust. Your feelings are deep and tender. You easily empathize with others, and have the ability to make very deep commitments.

Challenge: In your tendency to think in black and white terms, you can be an all-or-nothing thinker.

Challenge: You can become deeply focused and often tense, but focusing on a project or activity can also help you relax.

Challenge: When you are emotionally triggered, your energy can be read as icy or cool, just like an icicle or an iceberg— cold and immovable.

Challenge: You can be labeled a "know it all." What is funny is that this is a correct description of you, since your keenness and concise way of thinking does offer you the gift of knowing better than most about a lot of things!

COMMUNICATION

You value respect, loyalty, reliability, professionalism, appropriate humor, and timeliness in your communication with others.

You do not like being put on the spot spontaneously, but are eager to express yourself before a group if you have some purpose in view. You have a gift of being concise in your communication, and are able to share a lot of information clearly and in a few words. In short, you are brief but comprehensive.

You are quiet about your thoughts until you feel clear about your stance. You then have formed strong opinions about what is right or wrong, having a black and white opinion, with no gray areas. You may not always share your keen insight and strong opinions, as it depends on how worthy you feel your listening audience is.

When you have engaged in a conversation with another person, you give them your full attention and expect to be given the same when sharing your thoughts and feelings. You do not like being interrupted in the middle of sharing your stream of thought. It is very irritating to you, and it is especially irritating if you are intensely focused on a project or activity and someone tries to talk to you and interrupts you.

I have learned that it is difficult for my son Mark (TYPE 4^{SM} Energy) to give me his attention when he is concentrating on his computer, homework, mountain bikes, and any other activity he is focused on. If I try to engage him in a conversation spontaneously, I most likely will not get a response from him. If I keep persisting and push him to respond to me, he has a tendency to get upset and snap at me. A choice that is more honoring of him is to ask, "When can I talk to you?" He can reply to that, and together we create the structure he needs to shift tracks and give me his full attention when that time is right.

When asked a question, you expect the person who asked the question to pay attention to your answer. If the person doesn't pay close attention and asks the question again, the question seems redundant and superficial to you; therefore, you don't like to repeat yourself. You give your full attention to others and expect them to respond in kind when engaging in conversation with you.

> **Challenge:** You may sound critical or overly negative to others. You like to get to the essence as quickly as possible, and you can come across as blunt and too straightforward in expressing your opinions.

> **Challenge:** You can be too authoritative, bossy, or too condescending.

> **Challenge:** You may build walls around yourself so others cannot approach you, and they won't know how to talk to you.

> **Challenge:** You may be cold and distant, content to live in your own world, as it feels less painful to you when you have felt so misunderstood.

BEHAVIOR TENDENCIES

Your behavior tendencies express in a straightforward manner. You get to the bottom line as soon as you can in your approach to life, and you tend to stay on track, even when you move between tracks, or from one activity to another.

Relationships: You are a loyal and faithful friend, true to your word. If you make a promise, you keep it. It is your tendency to be self-sacrificing for the people with whom you are the closest. The more you feel you are being honored, the more easily you make who you are available to others, and even yourself.

Social: You do not form acquaintances readily. You are not the one who will be chatting with the person next to you in the grocery line; in fact, you probably think it does not make sense to do so when you don't even know the person! Rather, you prefer a narrow range of friends to whom you are very, very close and loyal.

You do not like to be spontaneously put in the spotlight. Ironically, your striking presence draws unwelcome attention to you.

Timeliness: The bottom line is, you are on time. Of the four Energy Types, you have the greatest tendency for timeliness. You take things literally and when someone says I will meet you at 4 o'clock, 4 o'clock means 4 o'clock. You take it personally and feel dishonored when the people you are closest to are consistently late.

Not long after my daughter Jenny (TYPE 1ˢᴹ Energy) and Tony (TYPE 4ˢᴹ Energy) were newly married, Tony had just started medical school. Tony took the bus and Jenny picked him up around the agreed-upon time of 5:00 p.m. In Jenny's words, "I would consistently get there late everyday. I was thinking that it was no big deal to be a little late. I really believed my timing was close enough." This happened for several weeks. One day she was 45 minutes late and things were getting tense. Tony finally had to talk about it. Tony shared with Jenny that it would mean a lot to him for her to be on time. He shared, "When we agreed on 5:00 p.m., I expect you to be here at 5:00 p.m." The bottom line for Tony was Jenny wasn't keeping her word, and it was personally offensive to Tony. Jenny admitted she was embarrassed, and didn't want to admit that she had dropped the ball so many times. "Once I realized how important it was for Tony and how important exactness and keeping your word was to him, I committed to always be on time," which she has done. This also demonstrates one valid motivation for conforming to the needs of others: The intent to honor another's Energy Type.

Work: You will thrive the most in a position that allows you to be your own authority. You have a natural tendency to stay on track with your work and to mentally organize yourself in such a way that you do not need an authority watching over you or micro-managing you. You quickly see what needs to be done and how to do it better than most.

When my son Mark (TYPE 4^{SM} Energy) was 17 years old, he started a successful eBay business selling used mountain bikes. I helped him learn how to set up and run an eBay business. He quickly learned what he needed to do to make it successful. He thoroughly enjoyed being his own boss.

One afternoon, I asked him if he was keeping accounting records of his sales and tracking his profits. He looked at me, somewhat irritated, and said "No, Mom, I am stupid. I am not doing any of that!" Of course, he was. He dominantly expresses TYPE 4^{SM} Energy! He definitely was blunt with me, yet understanding his TYPE 4^{SM} tendencies in his response, I did not take it personally. I simply responded, "Okay, that was blunt! My intention was to support you and see if you needed any help with that. I apologize if how I asked made you assume that I thought you didn't know what you were doing. Let me rephrase that: 'Is there anything I can help you with in your business, Mark?'" I also encouraged him to work on his tendency to be overly blunt and speak more respectfully, which he agreed to do. We both learned more about how to communicate effectively in honoring our very different natural tendencies.

Money: You are very thorough in how you plan your spending, and you tend to think things through before you spend your money. You prefer to save your money so you can invest in the best of what you want. You prefer to own less, but what you own needs to be of good quality and of value to you.

Physical Activity: You enjoy activities that require your ability to focus intensely and perfect your physical talents. You enjoy single sports and recreational pursuits. It makes sense that my son-in-law loves to rock climb. It is extreme, requires great focus, and one must be very thorough in the preparation and execution of the sport.

A physical activity that you have a unique tendency with is your experience of driving. You think you are the best driver on the road, and it bothers you that others don't understand and follow the rules of driving as well as you do. Your TYPE 4^{SM} tendencies can really manifest when you are driving, because you notice what you perceive as the weaknesses of other drivers, and you are not shy about sharing how you feel about such weaknesses in a blunt, opinionated way.

Another tendency I have noticed that is unique to your still and reflective nature is that you do not like to be rubbed or patted on your body in the same place over and over. You prefer a firm strong hug from a loved one over being stroked or repeatedly patted.

BODY LANGUAGE

You may or may not have a predominant amount of TYPE 4^{SM} Energy expressing through your body language and physical features. Most people are blended in their physical features, so you won't see

147

yourself in all these expressions, but you will notice that you have many expressions of TYPE 4^{SM} body language and physical features if you are a dominant TYPE 4^{SM} person.

Walking: You walk with little movement of your limbs and body in a very upright, still, stately manner.

Sitting/Standing: You sit very upright, with straight posture, both feet on the ground, hands folded or hanging on sides. Your sitting and standing could be called proper with a formal look. Most runway models express dominant TYPE 4^{SM} Energy—naturally erect, poised, and structured in movement with straight shoulders and perfect posture.

Voice/Language: A TYPE 4^{SM} voice is a lower pitch, with a clear, clean, smooth sound. You speak little but with a clear intent, using bold language. You say it how it is. Favorite words that you use frequently in your verbal expressions are: exactly, definitely, precisely, or perfect. You use phrases like, "That was stupid!" or "The meeting started at 11 o'clock, not 11:02." People who do voiceover work can tend to be TYPE 4^{SM} Energy as they have clear, precise, bold voices.

Doodling: You do not have a tendency to doodle—it's too much inefficient movement. However, you do tend to like to edit and proofread.

Personal Space: You like to keep things put away and out of sight, creating empty or negative space with no movement. You like your space to be clean, clear, and orderly.

Interior Design: TYPE 4^{SM} movement in interior design is what we call modern and contemporary. The design is simple and sleek with bold structures and décor.

"*Throughout my life, I had not enjoyed social situations. I felt like I had to force myself to be pleasant and make conversation. My parents tried to help me overcome this problem with even more social activities, books, tapes, etc. I would try to be fun, but it felt fake and gave me anxiety.*

"*I cried myself to sleep that first night after learning my Type. I felt like all those feelings and labels of "too picky, cold, unsocial, shy, quiet, critical" were confirmed.*

"*My husband felt like I was being put in a box. It was only after a few days of reflection and facing my stuff before I began to see the beauty and complex nature of a TYPE 4**SM [Energy]. It was not just okay to be still, it was perfect for me. The Energy Profiling model is the gift that allowed me to love me, the me that is constant, still, bold, precise.*

"*My interactions with others are more enjoyable now. No more trying to be what I thought others wanted. I live an authentic expression now. Others see that and get me for who I am. Understanding my truth lets others experience me in a way that is harmonious, honest, and honoring. Thank you, Carol!*"

—KALISTA WATSON (TYPE 4SM ENERGY),
DRESSING YOUR TRUTH EXPERT, UTAH

PHYSICAL FEATURES

Overall quality of your expression is sculpted, striking, and symmetrical. Your bone structure creates parallel lines and elongated ovals.

Skin and Skin Texture: TYPE 4SM skin is clear and reflective which gives it a porcelain, striking quality. This is due to the stillness in their being, which expresses as very small pores in their skin. All the models featured in skin care product commercials have TYPE 4^{SM} skin. It is not the skin care product that creates their porcelain skin; it is their stillness that expresses as naturally small pores.

I have TYPE 3^{SM} skin, a higher, more textured movement that expresses in my skin as hyper-pigmentation, more creases, and texture. I have come to learn that no skin care product can turn my skin into TYPE 4^{SM}, porcelain skin. It is easier working with the natural expression in my skin and bringing out the beauty in it, texture and all! TYPE 4^{SM} skin requires the least amount of upkeep to maintain its beauty. However, due to the small pore size, it is important to use a product that is water based and that hydrates the skin. Dryness is typically a problem.

Face Shape: Elongated oval, or rectangular with parallel lines on sides of face and across hairline. A widow's peak is a TYPE 4^{SM} feature, as it creates a point that divides the face into a mirror image of itself. The actress Courteney Cox is a good example of this. You could take one side of her face, and it would mirror perfectly the exact same features on the other side of her face.

Cheeks: Fast parallel lines, what we call high cheek bones

Nose: Two straight lines on side of nose bridge, sideways oval between nostrils, oval nostrils, and straight nose bridge

Eyebrows: Straight lines or half of elongated oval

Eyes: Oval

Hands: Very smooth, porcelain skin on top of the palm; parallel lines on sides of fingers; parallel lines on sides of nail beds; long fingers, often the same width all the way down the finger, creating parallel lines

FAMOUS PEOPLE

Women: Elizabeth Taylor, Courteney Cox, Natalie Portman, Jackie Onassis, Halle Barry, Jada Pinkett-Smith, Audrey Hepburn, Liv Tyler, Gwyneth Paltrow.

Men: Pierce Brosnan, Keanu Reeves, Johnny Depp, Tom Cruise, Sean Connery, John McCain, Elijah Wood, Michael Jordan, Jamie Foxx, Samuel L. Jackson

MUSIC AND MUSICIANS

Music that has low movement, is reflective, still, high contrast or bold, is TYPE 4^{SM} music. TYPE 4^{SM} music is also pure and precise and, when vocals are involved, you can actually hear the lyrics! Notable examples of TYPE 4^{SM} music are Ludwig von Beethoven's Fifth Symphony or Aaron Copeland's "Fanfare for the Common Man." A few TYPE 4^{SM} musicians include Josh Groban, White Stripes, Gwen Stefani, Enya, Celine Dion, Norah Jones, Vanessa Carlton, and David Archuleta.

NATIONS

Japan, France, England, and Germany have all historically been known to try and dominate through war. Switzerland and Finland have very TYPE 4^{SM} expressions in their culture.

"As a woman, and the CEO of an international company, I was extremely frustrated by the treatment I received, not just from men but also from women I met in association with our business. Rather than talking with me, they so often requested that they please talk with my husband, who was my partner. They couldn't imagine that I was actually the CEO. My talented husband and I had divided our duties, but I really did oversee everything.

However, I was often ignored or insulted by associates in our industry, and I admit that sometimes I chose to return an abrasive chain of words. That reaction certainly didn't help! Here I was, a sweet, mousy, frumpy person telling them what for and they didn't expect it nor did they like it.

"*When situations like that happened, I was so mad at myself for not being more flexible and kind. I hated the part of me that was so headstrong. Why couldn't I just be nice all of the time? So I tried the other path and when people insulted me or treated me poorly, I bit my tongue and stuffed my opinions and my anger. That caused havoc with my health, my marriage, and my happiness.*

"*When I met Carol, I was trying to be perfect at being everything TYPE 2*^{SM} *Energy is. Problem was, I absolutely could not do it. I felt like a failure. After I studied each energy and understood more fully what TYPE 2*^{SM} *Energy was, I knew without a doubt that it wasn't me. That was actually a huge relief. I was now on an adventure to find out who I really was.*

"*I attended one of Carol's events, and she brought the entire TYPE 1*^{SM} *Energy people together at the front of the audience. My sister was one of them! I was envious and wanted to be in that group with the bouncy, entertaining, laughing, quick-witted people. But as much as I love that energy, I knew right away it wasn't in my nature to be like that. So I thought I must be a TYPE 3*^{SM} *[Energy]. I get things done! I'm opinionated! But Carol wasn't convinced.*

"*I didn't even consider TYPE 4*^{SM} *Energy—it was perfectionist and judgmental and I thought that must be bad. But the more I studied what TYPE 4*^{SM} *Energy was, the more I began to see it in myself. The perfect way to load a dishwasher. The way I lined up my socks into columns and colors in my drawer. Seeing the big picture. Seeing people's potential. The judgments on others, and most especially, on myself. The way I liked to be alone sometimes. The way I sat completely straight. And, okay, my stubbornness.*

"And the stillness I had, even as a child. When I was 2 years old, I sat on the bottom shelf in a store right among the life-sized dolls, wearing my fashionable winter coat and hat. A lady shopper was examining all of the dolls carefully, deciding which to buy. I sat there very still, but when she got close to touch me I jumped up and ran away. She screamed!

"After contemplating all of this, I was hit by the brightest and most wonderful light! I had a dominant TYPE 4^{SM} Energy! It was the most freeing, amazing, lifting feeling I had ever known. I love knowing who I am! Now I understand why I think, walk, talk and act the way I do. And guess what? It's okay! It's fabulous! Now I can enter a room or stand at a trade show and I receive respect. Why? I think it's because I am living more closely to the way I was made to be. People seem to be aware that I know what I want and I am rarely ignored or insulted. That frees me up and allows me to actually be more kind. I'm not turning cartwheels to try to get my way. I don't have to be abrasive because I have learned to use my energy without even speaking. Somehow others know who I am—my energy conveys it. Now that I have learned about my weaknesses, I've worked diligently to not be so hard on others and on myself. And I don't have to be right. I now know how to better approach my children and husband. I am also better at communicating with our customers. And I have strengths! My opinions are strong, and that's great! I have an incredible sense of direction or gut feeling when it comes to making business decisions. I've helped improve our products and that brings me great joy! I feel and think deeply.

"I went from loathing myself for not being what I thought I should be, to accepting and loving myself for what I am and what I have to offer. Basically, I've learned that I'm okay, and that's

made a world of difference. Thanks, Carol Tuttle! You have completely changed my life. I'll be forever grateful to you."

—SHERYL LAUKAT (TYPE 4ᔆᴹ ENERGY), CEO,
CANNONBALL MUSICAL INSTRUMENTS

HOW YOUR ENERGY AFFECTS OTHER PEOPLE

Your energy creates an ambience of clearness and stability. Your constant, still energy quiets the people around you. You are naturally a stabilizing force to the rest of us. When you feel like other people are cool to you, their demeanor is actually showing respect for the authoritative, reflective qualities you emanate.

At times, others can feel you are unapproachable, inaccessible, or rigid. It would be smart for you to know that it works well for you to initiate interaction with others. When you are uncomfortable or disturbed, you move into a state of more stillness and your constant, still energy can come across to other Energy Types as rigid and icy.

As you are conscious of your natural movement and are more aware of who you interact with, you will be able to manage yourself in a way that supports others in being in rapport with you. As you stay conscious of and love who you are, rather than judge your natural movement, you will be consistently aligned with your core true nature and others will always enjoy being around you.

FOR OTHERS: CREATING A SUCCESSFUL RELATIONSHIP WITH A DOMINANT TYPE 4ᔆᴹ PERSON

DOs

Respect them as their own authority. Know that their true nature—the natural movement expressed through them—is clear, concise, simple, structured and bold! As you accept that, you accept them. Know they have a respect for privacy and a respect for personal space. They consistently need time alone to process their thoughts and feelings, and to get clear on where they stand on things that matter to them.

DON'Ts

Don't embarrass them in front of others! Don't tell them what to do and how to do it, rather engage them in a conversation to invite them to share how they see and feel about things. Don't judge them to be too cool, too serious, too literal. It is their constant, still energy you are experiencing. Don't say things like, "You are too serious," "You take things too literally," "Lighten up!" or, "Loosen up. You are too uptight!" Don't touch their stuff without asking.

Don't set yourself up to be disappointed by placing on them your expectations of how you (in your Energy Type) would move through life, and what you would do to get from point A to point B. TYPE 4^{SM} people move in a very straightforward line, very rarely veering off track from their goal.

At the young age of 12, my son Mark (TYPE 4^{SM} Energy) came to me and asked me how to run the washing machine. He wanted his clothes done exactly the way he wanted them, so learning how to wash them himself was the best solution in his mind. I have noticed it is a common tendency for those who express TYPE 4^{SM} Energy to be particular about their laundry, and to manage their clothing with care and precision. Their keen eye for having things exact gives them sensitivity to wanting their laundry folded exactly. For example, if they were folding sheets they would want all the corners to match precisely; if they were folding shirts they would notice if the shirt was not folded symmetrically.

When Mark was about 17, he came to me asking me not to dry his shirts on such a hot setting because he did not want them to shrink. Because of my TYPE 3^{SM} Energy, I tend to do things swiftly, wanting to get the job done without paying keen attention to some details. Evidently, I was not matching Mark's expectations. He had reminded me several times, to no avail. One day I walked into the laundry room and saw the following written boldly and clearly with a marker on our dryer, "Do not use this setting. Use this one!"

Knowing my son's tendencies because of his TYPE 4^{SM} Energy, I took this bold form of communication in a very heartfelt way. I did not get upset or think it was inappropriate. Rather, I felt a sense of appreciation for who he is and had the pleasure of pleasantly being reminded of this every time I did the laundry!

My son Mario (TYPE 1^{SM} Energy) and his girlfriend (TYPE 4^{SM} Energy) both decided to start college. They had been working and spending their free time socializing and hanging out with friends. The opportunity to go to college was very timely for both of them. Mario's girlfriend saw this opportunity in a very black and white way as a once-in-a-lifetime opportunity that she did not want to "blow."

With her 4-ness, she became very business-like about the opportunity and wanted to make sure that everything in her life supported her in staying on track and not getting distracted. She told Mario she needed to see him less and make school her priority. Due to her all-or-nothing nature, she at first thought, "Maybe I have to stop seeing him altogether and give my full attention to school, because if I am going to succeed I can't afford to be distracted and lose my focus."

I helped her by suggesting she give herself some time to come up with a plan. The plan would create the structure she needed to give the appropriate time to school and also include Mario. With her tendency for perfection and wanting to do her very best, she knew she needed to allow herself the right to create that with her schooling. I suggested she get into school and allow herself time to have a keener sense of how much time it would require and what would best support her, and to then include in her schedule the amount of play time she felt comfortable with.

People who express TYPE 4^{SM} Energy are very focused and tend to have one-track minds. My son-in-law Tony (TYPE 4^{SM} Energy) is in medical school and that is his primary "track" right now. He dedicates his time and priorities to being the best med student he can be. My daughter Jenny (TYPE 1^{SM} Energy) understands this about Tony, that it is not in his nature to be able to diversify his life much with such a huge commitment as med school that requires outstanding commitment.

People who express dominant TYPE 4^{SM} Energy do not like being distracted when focused. It is very irritating to be distracted from the task at hand. Knowing this about yourself allows you to create more reasonable expectations of yourself and of the people you are in relationships with.

A person with TYPE 4^{SM} Energy requires structure and focus, a one-track approach to larger commitments in life. In your mind, it would be ridiculous to commit so much time and money to something without demanding perfection from yourself. You don't understand how anyone could do it any different.

Both Jenny and Mario, with their TYPE 1^{SM} Energy, are very adaptable people. Their nature allows them to connect and disconnect readily to most situations. But Tony and Mario's girlfriend move from track to track. When they are on school track, that is their single focus. When they have satisfied their commitment with school and allowed themselves a play track, they create a start and end time to their playtime track. Knowing they will get back on track with school actually allows them to let down and have fun and not think about school while they are on their play track.

Both Jenny and Mario can easily adapt to their partners' natures and support them without feeling compromised. The demand for structure in their TYPE 4^{SM} partners can actually help them add more structure to their lifestyle. The one thing they have to watch is to not let the structure overtake them. A person with TYPE 1^{SM} Energy needs to allow spontaneity within structure to honor their own true nature.

"I would love to tell you and whoever will listen about how knowing my Energy Type has helped me in my life... I am a 4/1 and having that knowledge gives me a confidence boost in the way I show myself to the world. Before I knew my type, I wasn't fully living the truth of myself. Now I act as if everything I do and say is acceptable because that is how a 4 can act. However, that isn't to be confused as thinking I am always right. Haha.

"Another benefit of understanding Energy Types is knowing what kind of girls I date. After learning the program I realized almost every girl I have dated is a 1/4. I am most attracted to this energy combination. So when I meet new girls and I am considering dating them it is helpful to know what kind of energy they are. I also dress my truth according to the guidelines you have set and I feel confident and attractive and secure in my clothing choices.

"Another thing that comes to mind in knowing Energy Types— my family and especially my mother know what to expect from me and my mother knows how to get me to do something... It has strengthened our relationship."

—BRANDON LAUKAT, (TYPE 4^{SM} ENERGY)

"Thank you for the opportunity to share my Energy Profiling story. As a result of attending an Energy Profiling workshop, I feel a confidence and sureness about myself that had previously eluded me. You see, I had been living as a TYPE 2^{SM} Energy my entire adult life. Even in the workshop after the Energy Types were taught and we were asked to divide ourselves into the group we thought we were in, I put myself into the TYPE 2^{SM} group.

Later we learned that many women take on the energy of their upbringing.

"The facilitator came around and immediately could see by my physical characteristics that I was in the wrong group and she asked me to step into the TYPE 4ᴹ (earth) group. Well, when I stepped into the TYPE 4ᴹ group, I magically felt a shift in my energy. I say magically, because it really happened that fast, at the blink of an eye. I felt happy, elated even. You see, all my life I have been quiet and introverted, and took it as being shy. But in reality, I am not shy, just quiet by nature, which is a characteristic of the constant, still energy of the TYPE 4ᴹ [movement]… With the shift came a whopping 'Ah-ha!' as in, 'Now that's why I'm like that' and 'Now this is the real me.'

"After the workshop, I was giddy for weeks. I integrated the information fairly quickly and today, six months afterwards, I am still grateful every day for what I learned. I am stronger and more confident and, more importantly, kinder and more tolerant toward others.

"Thank you for the gift of your Energy Profiling system, Carol. Thank you for helping me and many others feel better about ourselves. I just can't say enough good about it.

"Many, many blessings, love, peace and joy to you and yours."
—NORA BOW (TYPE 4ᴹ ENERGY), WASHINGTON

SUMMARY OF THE DOMINANT TYPE 4ᴹ PERSON – CONSTANT, STILL ENERGY

Carbon/earth is TYPE 4ᴹ Energy. People in this category have an energy that is constant and still. These people are reflective and thorough with an unerring eye for perfecting things. Their dominant shape in physical features is a straight line, visible in the parallel lines on the sides of their face, straight hairline, and their typically erect posture.

As a person who expresses dominant TYPE 4^{SM} Energy, you may have a tendency toward these strengths:

- You move in a direct, straightforward line from Point A to Point B. In this manner you accomplish many tasks.

- You are poised and still with very little movement, and you have a regal countenance.

- You are clear and precise in your language and manner.

- You have laser-like mental focus.

- You have a quietness and serenity about you that speaks volumes.

- You are stable and consistent. People can trust you.

- You easily follow and obey rules, if you trust the source of those rules or if you feel that following them will lead you to a greater end.

- You have a keen eye that sees clearly what needs to be done to improve, perfect, and streamline things, and make it so others can reproduce it in a cost-effective manner.

- You are contemplative and seek more knowledge and wisdom.

- You are a pillar of strength and can anchor all those who surround you.

- You are captivating and mesmerizing and reflect to others an air of sophistication.

- You stay on track when you start something; it's important to finish what you start.

As a person who expresses dominant TYPE 4^{SM} Energy, you may have a tendency towards these challenges:

- You may be cold and distant, content to live in your own world, building emotional walls around you so others do not approach you or know how to talk to you.

- You can seem too authoritative, bossy, or condescending.

- You may appear harsh, judgmental, or too opinionated.

- You can get stuck in perfecting things, bringing your forward movement to a standstill.

TYPE 4^{SM} WORD PORTRAIT

Articulate	Contrasting	Exact
Astute	Cool	Explicit
Black & white	Courtly	Firm
Bold	Decisive	Focused
Blunt	Defined	Formal
Calculated	Definite	Frosty
Calm	Deliberate	Icy
Captivating	Debonair	Impressive
Chic	Dignified	In control
Classic	Dignity	Incisive
Clean	Diplomatic	Independent
Clear	Discreet	Inscrutable
Commanding	Distinctive	Keen
Competent	Distinguished	Kingly
Concise	Dramatic	Lavish
Conservative	Efficient	Levelheaded
Consistent	Elite	Luminous
Contemplative	Enchanting	Magnificent
Contemporary	Enticing	Majestic

Meditative	Self-contained	Straightforward
Mesmerizing	Self-reliant	Striking
Modern	Serene	Stunning
Mysterious	Serious	Stylized
Neat	Sleek	Suave
Noble	Smooth	Tailored
Notable	Sophisticated	Thorough
One-track Mind	Stark	Timely
Opulent	Stately	Tranquil
Perceptive	Statuesque	Undisturbed
Perfectionist	Staunch	Valiant
Placid	Stay on Track	Vivid
Poised	Stern	Vogue
Polished	Still	Well-structured
Polite	Stillness	
Precise		
Private		
Professional		
Profound		
Proper		
Point A to Point B		
Quality		
Queenly		
Refined		
Reflective		
Regal		
Reserved		
Respectful		
Restrained		
Satin		

PART

The Gift of Wholeness within the Four Energy Types

WITH THE NATURAL GIFT AND TALENTS of each Energy Type, we create a picture of wholeness. For a recap, TYPE 1^{SM} Energy initiates the cycle of wholeness by coming up with new ideas and the inspiration and hope of the possibility of making them come true. TYPE 2^{SM} Energy leads to questions to gather the details necessary to have a steady plan that will make the ideas work. TYPE 3^{SM} Energy pushes the plans through to create a result. And the keen eye that comes with TYPE 4^{SM} Energy can observe the whole process as well as the result. They see what is missing and what could be made better to deliver the completed whole to the world with a smooth system that can be duplicated.

We have all four energies expressing through us, yet it is our dominant Energy Type that adds value to the wholeness of humanity. Consider the possibility that we created our human experience in this way in order to support us in learning through partnership and unity, working as a whole rather than independently. There are many times in life we have to be willing to play all the roles that the movement of each Energy Type offers us. But life becomes more balanced as we recognize our natural gifts and invite partnerships and support from others who, by sharing their natural gifts and talents with us, help to create life as a whole experience.

The following is a fun way to see how each Energy Type would respond to the same situation. Let's pretend there are a group of

40 people, with representations of all four Energy Types within the group. They live in the state of New York on the east coast of the United States in the mid-nineteenth century. The group decides they want to cross the plains in covered wagons to start a new life on the west coast of the country. Our initial reaction says a lot about what Energy Type we are.

The group members with TYPE 1^{SM} Energy would be very excited about the adventure ahead; their initial comment would be, "Oh boy, let's go!"

Those with dominant TYPE 2^{SM} Energy would start asking themselves the following questions: "That is a big undertaking—what do we need to do to prepare to go? What do we need to leave behind? How can I part with that? What will we need during the journey? What will we need when we get there? Are you sure you want to do this? Am I sure I want to do this? Why am I doing this anyway?"

Those with dominant TYPE 3^{SM} Energy would ask, "What day do we want to get to our destination?" and knowing that, they would work backwards to determine what needed to be done, making sure that they accomplish their goals. During the journey, they would be the ones to organize the wagons and make sure all the jobs were getting done along the trail.

The people with dominant TYPE 4^{SM} Energy would think deeply about the validity of needing to move to the West Coast, and if they did not feel there was a valid reason, would say, "I am not leaving New York!"

Here is a fun and helpful summary of each Energy Type's part in the experience of wholeness.

NATURAL ESSENCE OF EACH ENERGY TYPE'S NATURAL MOVEMENT

- TYPE 1^{SM} Energy—Lightness

- TYPE 2^{SM} Energy—Connectedness

- TYPE 3^{SM} Energy—Sureness

- TYPE 4^{SM} Energy—Exactness

THE GIFT AND TALENT OF EACH ENERGY TYPE

- TYPE 1^{SM} Energy: Coming up with new ideas and the inspiration and hope of the possibility of making them come true.

- TYPE 2^{SM} Energy: Asking the questions to gather the details necessary to have a steady plan that will make the ideas work.

- TYPE 3^{SM} Energy: Pushing the plans through to create a result.

- TYPE 4^{SM} Energy: Observing the whole process and the result with a keen eye to see what is missing and what could be made better to deliver the completed whole to the world in a smooth system that can be easily duplicated.

THE PHRASE THAT RECOGNIZES THE GIFT AND TALENT OF EACH ENERGY TYPE

- TYPE 1^{SM} Energy: "I have a new idea and we can do it."

- TYPE 2^{SM} Energy: "What do we need to know and do to make the idea possible?"

- TYPE 3^{SM} Energy: "Let's get to work and get it done!"

- TYPE 4^{SM} Energy: "Here is how we can make it better, and here is how we can duplicate it."

WHAT IS IMPORTANT FOR EACH ENERGY TYPE TO MAINTAIN LIFE BALANCE

- TYPE 1^{SM} Energy: That you have fun and keep it light.

- TYPE 2^{SM} Energy: To allow yourself to ask questions and know the details.

- TYPE 3^{SM} Energy: To get the job done.

- TYPE 4^{SM} Energy: That you respect your need to be right and exact.

HOW EACH ENERGY TYPE PROCESSES INFORMATION

- TYPE 1^{SM} Energy: Quick and spontaneous. They process information quickly so others may perceive them as not thinking things through. They can often interrupt or change the topic mid-sentence because they process information so much faster than other people do.

- TYPE 2^{SM} Energy: Slower and methodical. They have a continuous process of interconnected thought. They always connect the past to the now which then connects to the future.

- TYPE 3^{SM} Energy: Swift and deliberate. They compartmentalize their thoughts to keep track of all the activities they have put into motion.

- TYPE 4^{SM} Energy: Still and precise. They think in black-and-white terms, take in a lot of information and quickly figure out what has value and what does not. They can be all-or-nothing thinkers.

COMMON EXPRESSIONS WE SHARE WITH EACH ENERGY TYPE THAT CONFLICT WITH THEIR NATURAL MOVEMENT

Each Type is told:

- TYPE 1^{SM} Energy: "Settle down." "Stop moving around so much." "You are too old for that." "It's hard for me to take you seriously." "You are so cute!"

- TYPE 2^{SM} Energy: "Hurry up!" "Come on, come on, come on!" "Why don't you just make up your mind?" "Stop asking so many questions." "You are so fussy about details!"

- TYPE 3^{SM} Energy: "Why can't you just relax?" "Slow down. Take it easy!" "You are so fast!"

- TYPE 4^{SM} Energy: "Lighten up." "Loosen up." "Don't be so serious all the time." "You are so thorough."

LEADERSHIP TENDENCIES FOR EACH ENERGY TYPE

- TYPE 1^{SM} Energy: Encouraging and uplifting. Others are motivated because they are having so much fun.

- TYPE 2^{SM} Energy: Connecting and guiding. Others are motivated because they know they feel understood and are cared about.

- TYPE 3^{SM} Energy: Motivating and pushing forward. Others are motivated because the vision of the result inspires them.

- TYPE 4^{SM} Energy: Authoritative and steady. Others are motivated because they feel respected and honored.

These characteristics help us to recognize and see the wholeness that the four Energy Types comprise. While we lead with a given Energy Type, no one dominant energy can be complete standing by itself. Each Energy Type needs to be supported by the others—we need each other!

Your primary Energy Type forms the foundation of who you are, and your secondary Energy Type plays an important role in supporting you. Your third and fourth energies add uniqueness to who you are so that you are completely individual.

For example, my profile is a 3-4-1-2. I express a dominant TYPE 3^{SM} Energy. I definitely move through life swiftly, loving to get the job done, leaving a lasting impression. My secondary is a TYPE 4^{SM} Energy and I express the qualities of my 4-ness in my gift of having a keen eye, taking in the bigger picture and seeing how we can make a smooth system that can be duplicated. I know TYPE 4^{SM} is not my dominant expression because I do not move through life in a precise linear manner, but I have many qualities of expression that are TYPE 4^{SM} Energy. I follow my TYPE 4^{SM} Energy with my TYPE 1^{SM} Energy. I can come up with some amazing ideas and I can have a lot of fun, yet this quality of expression is not what I lead with. I have discovered that my closest friends are dominant TYPE 1^{SM} people. I enjoy being with them when I choose to play or recreate, as they really bring the playfulness out in me. The least expressive movement in me is my TYPE 2^{SM} Energy. I am not a detailed person when it comes to a lot of things in my life. I am a very caring, loving, generous person, but I express those qualities in the movement of my more dominant energies.

As I said in the beginning of this book, I am not going to provide you with a multiple-choice question assessment test. It's so easy to figure out where tests like those are going with the choices you are given, you could easily manipulate the answers so that the results are what you think you want them to be.

Vibration and movement, and how they are expressed in our human tendencies and our body language and physical features, are the best measurement of knowing your true nature. They are more honest than we are! I guarantee that if you are ready to live your truth, your truth is going to be delivered to you on a silver platter.

Why is it so important to embrace your Energy Type and live true to your nature?

When any of us at tempt to operate outside of our own natural movement, our lives go out of balance and things start to go wrong. Frustrations that we chalk up to circumstance or bad luck can often be explained and resolved by identifying how we live contrary to our true natures. If you currently experience a challenge in a certain area of your life, consider the possibility that you are fighting against your true nature in those scenarios. Consider which area of your life you most need to improve and read the rest of this section with the intent to improve by living true to your natural expression.

"As I grew up I was pushed more into my secondary Energy Type. In fact I got so far away from my Energy Type I ended up in a career doing software development. I was a software developer without an eye for details. Ha ha.

"I wish I could say that after finding out I was a TYPE 1^{SM} my life fell into place. But, it takes time to re-learn how to be myself. While I am working to get out of software development, I have found ways to bring a TYPE 1^{SM} Energy to my job. I try to keep myself doing more creative or design things. I also make sure that I am often learning new things. Awesome!

"I used to feel like I would be trapped developing software forever. Now I see that it is temporary and will help me get to where I want to be. I have so many ideas I want to do. I have books to write, speaking to do, people to train, a world changing organization to build, and take a try at acting. My story is still being written, but knowing what my natural strengths are helps me focus in the right way."

—KEITH BROWN (TYPE 1^{SM} ENERGY)

STRENGTHEN YOUR RELATIONSHIPS AND MARRIAGE

When you feel extended strain in a relationship or marriage, chances are, one or the other of you is not living true to your nature or honoring the other in their true nature. Learning and accepting your Energy Type can actually be a monumental step in resolving marital conflict and redefining a relationship in a way that's more mutually supportive.

My husband Jonathan and I have had many frustrations in our own marriage, due to not understanding and having the awareness to honor each other's very different movement and nature.

The Energy Profiling system and knowing our different Energy Types has made a world of difference for us. Jonathan is more methodical and enjoys going over details. He needs to ask more questions to gather those details, and this makes it more comfortable for him to move forward.

On the other hand, I move through life with more swiftness and sureness, taking care of details as I go along.

For years I tried to make him more like me and he tried to make me more like him. That ended in a lot of frustration and confusion on how to move forward more easily together. We have learned that we both need to allow each other to do it our own way at times. As was stated earlier in the book, the Energy Profiling system taught me that people, like things in nature, come with built-in features that are meant to be permanent. For example, it's impossible to change a willow tree into an evergreen tree, no matter how much I hack and trim and wire-up the branches. It will still want to grow in its own flowing, downward-curving manner, never being able to change to the rigid upward-stillness of a pine.

As you live your true nature, you support others in living theirs. Recently, we took a trip to Colorado for a training we wanted to attend. We knew we would arrive late. On the airplane, Jonathan realized the event was at a different hotel than we originally thought and that there would not be a shuttle service we could use for transportation. At that point, we decided we needed to rent a car.

I was concerned about being even later. I wanted to get a rental car as quickly as we could, and not worry about price. My priority was getting there. Jonathan's priority was to find the lowest price and to go to several rental counters to gather the details to know which car agency to use.

Rather than argue with him and try to convince him to change his mind, I said, "I know it is important for you to gather all that information. What is important to me right now is getting there quickly, so I am going to go to the nearest rental agency and, if I feel the price is reasonable, I am going to go ahead and rent a car and get going. You can come with me, or go about it in a way that honors you."

He was a little dumbfounded by my remark. He felt discomfort about moving into this decision so quickly, had the choice of judging it as unacceptable, and then agreed to go with my approach.

It was a beautiful opportunity to experience that neither one of us had the better way. On our ride over to our event, we discussed our difference in approach and had the benefit of added insight to how our different Energy Types were the driving force behind these different approaches.

We have been able to create a very strong friendship and support system in our marriage, thanks to the insights and expanded awareness given us through the Energy Profiling model. As you apply what you've learned about your Energy Type to your relationships, you will have insights and a-ha's, as well. What you do with them is up to you!

UNDERSTAND YOUR FAMILY BETTER

When you understand your own Energy Type and how it compares to your family members' Energy Types, you are likely to be more understanding, patient, and forgiving. If your family is experiencing conflict lately, don't just go to the root of the problem—get to the root of the energy. Whose nature is not being honored? Who in the family has a need that's not being met?

It's valuable to understand the Energy Types of everyone in your family. You will all naturally express your energy whether you realize it or not. For example, my daughter Anne (TYPE 2^{SM} Energy) came home from an outing one day and shared with me, "I saw a TYPE 3^{SM} mom changing her baby's diaper. She did it swiftly and with determination. It made me think that in your nurturing and caring for me, your movement was just like that mom's. It seemed familiar to me."

MOVE UP IN YOUR CAREER

Success naturally comes to those people who live in harmony with their true nature. That's because people living in balance with their natural movement are also in balance with their greatest gifts and talents, which they bring to the workplace.

If you've ever felt like being recognized or respected at work was a challenge, you may have been trying to be someone you're not. Allow your co-workers, supervisors, and employees experience the gift of the true you. If you express dominant TYPE 1^{SM} Energy, bring lightness along to your next meeting. If you express dominant TYPE 2^{SM} Energy, embrace your ability to bring calm connectedness to a situation. If you express dominant TYPE 3^{SM} Energy, let loose with your encouragement for others. If you express dominant TYPE 4^{SM} Energy, share the respect that you expect to receive. I'm excited for what will show up for you in your career as you live true to your nature.

FREE YOURSELF

Don't wait for permission to be who you are. As you allow yourself to live true to who you are, all aspects of your life come into more harmony to support you in the journey that is perfect for you. Trust what has already happened in your life to be the perfect experience for you, and the experience you are having now to be perfect as well.

I always say if it wasn't what was perfect for you, then something else would be happening!

I was recently getting my hair done at our Dressing Your Truth Hair Salon when our stylist's next client, Diane, arrived early. Diane had recently come to an Energy Profiling class then quickly signed up for Dressing Your Truth, which is typical for her TYPE 3^{SM} Energy (get it going and get it done). I asked her what the last two months had been like for her, as it was apparent that she had undergone a massive transformation. She said people were amazed by how great she looked and curious about what she had done. She shared with me that her transformation in her appearance was incredibly magnificent but, more importantly, her inner transformation was profound. In her words she shared, "I feel like I was let out of prison, a prison I didn't know I was in for all these years."

If you're still not certain about your Energy Type, reflect on the Word Portraits at the end of each Energy Type's section. You will find the majority of words reflect the movement and expression of each dominant Energy Type. If you feel a certain Energy Type speaking to you, yet your Body Profile does not match the other aspects of the dominant Energy Type you think you are, look for similar words on the Word Portrait sheet that matches your Body Profile. Our bodies consistently express our dominant Energy Type when our personalities may vary from this expression. I say, go with what your body tells you, rather than your personality. As you trust this and allow yourself to be the Energy Type your body tells you that you are, you will see qualities emerge that are truly you, qualities that you actually expressed earlier in your life.

"Carol Tuttle's Energy Profiling system has been one of the most incredible experiences of my life. I've spent years doing energy work, observing, shifting and healing myself from the inside out as

well as helping others free themselves. Yet the transformation that occurred as I went through the Energy Profiling course completed that certain something that was missing in my search.

"Learning... and beginning to live my Energy Type was a profound transformation, an honoring of my true energy and being, an aligning of the inside with the outside, a coming home to who I truly am— even to feeling at home in my body for the first time in my life. It has allowed me to be in alignment with who I am, feel it on the inside and show it to the exterior world. It has allowed me to step into my own power gracefully and in a way that allows me to accept and honor others. Besides, it is delightful when you have your core being recognized and appreciated by others. It is an experience that is so luscious, so delicious, so comforting and true.

"I realize that the transformation continues even after months of learning my Energy Type. I'm a TYPE 3^{SM} [Energy] with a secondary TYPE 2^{SM} [Energy]. I feel fabulous. I look magnificent. My business is growing significantly. I'm more prosperous. I'm having so much fun with it all. I feel happier, more content, more relaxed. It is a transformation that is not a one time thing, but something that expands as I continue to live my core truth, the vibration that honors me. I'm excited to watch my own progress.

"Knowing my element, movement, and vibration makes such a difference in the way I walk in the world. It is truly the best gift I've given myself."

—DEBORAH MILLER, PH.D., (TYPE 3^{SM} ENERGY), MEXICO

"*Thank you, Carol for giving myself and many others a chance to learn life by giving the knowledge that leads us to discover the truth within us. Throughout my life, it seemed like I have always needed permission. I felt like I needed permission from someone in my life to do what I wanted to do. I remember after my divorce, a dear friend said to me, 'It's all right if you do [such-and-such].' I felt all right because it was really something that I wanted to do and I felt happy that she said it was okay. But the thought that stayed in my mind was, 'Why do I need permission from someone before I can do what I want to do?'*

"*In our class last summer, an awesome lady voiced my thoughts, 'I just needed permission. No one ever told me before that I could. It's all right for me to think and feel like I do.' Wow! It was amazing to have someone sitting next to me voice the same thoughts that I had struggled with all my life! Many times during that special class, sweet, cleansing tears were shed, as were many moments filled with joyous laughter and applause in recognition of our newly learned gifts and abilities within ourselves. Learning about my Energy Type actually gave me permission to be me. Thank you, Carol, for being the permission-giver to so many!*"

—ALY'CE (TYPE 1^{SM} ENERGY), WASHINGTON

THE YIN AND YANG OF THE ENERGY TYPES

I HAVE ALREADY INTRODUCED YOU to the quality of Yin Yang movement as it expresses in nature. Here is a quick review:

In Chinese philosophy, the concept of Yin Yang is used to describe how seemingly opposing forces are interdependent in the natural world. Yin Yang refers to opposite expressions. Yin is usually characterized as slow, soft, insubstantial, diffuse, cold, wet, and tranquil. It is generally associated with the feminine, birth and generation, and with the night. Yang, by contrast, is characterized as hard, fast, solid, dry, focused, hot, and aggressive. It is generally associated with masculinity and daytime.

In the model of Energy Profiling, Yin Yang takes on an important role to support us in living our true nature. Historically, in our culture, the movement that is identified as yin has been deemed a feminine movement and the yang has been deemed a masculine movement. We have a cultural cookie-cutter mold that suggests that all women should lead with a dominant yin movement, which is soft, and that men should lead with a dominant yang movement, which is aggressive.

Years ago, I started my marriage with this as my subconscious reference point on how to move forward as a woman in my adult life. It didn't help matters that I had a TYPE 2^{SM}/1^{SM} mom who supported this reference of how to be a woman, and a dominant TYPE 3^{SM}/4^{SM} dad, along with two of my three brothers who expressed TYPE 3^{SM} and TYPE 4^{SM} Energies. Well, to make a long story short, I expected my husband to be the yang movement, to be aggressive and go after life "like a man." He expected me to be the soft, nurturing wife who loved to cuddle and speak softly! We have been married 30 years, and it wasn't until 26 years into our marriage, when I started to develop the Energy Profiling system, that we discovered one of the primary reasons our marriage had been such a challenge: I had an underlying belief that I was supposed to be a TYPE 2^{SM} woman.

I was never successful at it. I just frustrated myself, feeling that was the way women were supposed to be, and I constantly pushed Jonathan to be a TYPE 3^{SM}/4 man, because I thought that was the way men were supposed to be. We had it all backwards. For all those years, we tried to make each other more like ourselves. It is hilarious to me now, looking back, that even in my trying to be a 2, I was really being true to my TYPE 3^{SM} nature by pushing him!

It is time to strip the old paradigms of what we relate to as feminine and masculine qualities. The Energy Profiling system gives us permission to be the natural expression of our God-given selves. I am a very yang, yang woman. Which means, in my TYPE 3^{SM}/4 energy, I am a very dynamic and bold woman. There is not a whole lot of softness in my natural expression. My husband is a very yin, yin male. Which means in his TYPE 2^{SM}/1 energy, he is a very subtle and playful man. We fully recognize our natures now and are both living in them, which has helped us to completely turn our marriage around. Knowing our Energy Types has allowed us to strip our minds of unreasonable expectations that were based on cultural models of women and men that no longer serve us.

"I was absolutely enthralled the first time that I heard Carol introduce the Energy Profiling system at a workshop. I had been familiar with several different methods of typing people, and have even used them in teaching my own workshops, but none of them

ever seemed to work 100 percent for me personally. I found them valuable, but lacking.

"I have studied Eastern health modalities and religions and feel that they have tremendous insights into people's energy and how it affects behavior. In the most inspired way, Carol has integrated many disparate pieces of Eastern and Western thought into an amazingly accurate whole. Her Energy Profiling system is simple, elegant, and accurate.

"I live in a culture that usually places value on women in one of the four Energy Types (TYPE 2^{SM} [Energy], taking care of details, being organized, sitting to the side of the "main" action) and that is not my Energy Type or even my secondary! When I learned about my authentic Energy Type (TYPE 3^{SM} Energy) and found out how and why I think and act the way that I do, I knew I would never have to try to fit into anyone else's idea of what I should be ever again. I felt free to just be me, letting the chips fall where they may.

"It has been an interesting transformation. As I've been standing in my truth and acting in authenticity, other people react universally with acceptance. In the past, I unconsciously tried to be something that I'm not (TYPE 2^{SM} Energy), and it felt awkward and ill-fitting to me which made others around me uncomfortable. Now that I'm living in my true energy, I am at ease, which puts others at ease. How cool is that?

"Because the Energy Profiling information is so simple, it is pretty easy to read other people. I understand my husband and my mostly-grown children much better, and no longer see them as frustrating or uncooperative, just living in their true energy. As I honor that and allow them to live in their authenticity, they relax and are more cooperative. Who could've seen that coming? It's an upward spiral of family harmony!"

—BETH YOUNG (TYPE 3^{SM} ENERGY), UTAH

I Don't Like My Energy Type!

WHEN I STARTED WRITING THIS BOOK, I sent an email out to the hundreds of people who had come to an Energy Profiling class, inviting them to share their Energy Profiling stories with me. I was curious about how much it had impacted their day-to-day lives. I asked them to share how knowing their Energy Type had made a difference in understanding themselves and others, and improved the overall quality of their lives.

I was amazed by how many people I heard from, and the stories were remarkable. I noticed a theme: The people I heard from were primarily those who initially did not like their dominant Energy Type when they found out what it was.

As you have read the stories in this book, you may have noticed this theme. This book and information are sorely needed to help people sort things out! I know I lived in my secondary TYPE 4^{SM} Energy a lot, a lot while growing up. In my family, I experienced a father who was unpredictable in his mood swings, and a mother who constantly tried to keep us all from upsetting my dad. So my dominant TYPE 3^{SM} Energy was too rambunctious for my dad, and I learned to stay quiet and still a lot, to not rock the boat, or be too much because it might make my dad mad. Does this seem at all familiar to you?

I hid my true nature a lot during my childhood, because that is what we do as kids. We hide from being ourselves, and we hide in our secondary Energy Type. For me, that was a TYPE 4^{SM} Energy; for my husband, that was a TYPE 1^{SM} Energy. Jonathan expresses dominant

TYPE 2^{SM} Energy, but somewhere along the timeline (we think it was in his junior high school days), he started to act more from his TYPE 1^{SM} Energy. In his mind, he thought that would make him popular to be cute and funny. He acted like he expressed dominant TYPE 1^{SM} Energy in all his social settings. We both brought the tendencies to hide out in our secondary Energy Type into our marriage.

What has been interesting to notice is that when either one of us defaults to our secondary Energy Type, and we are not truly being ourselves, it triggers the other one to go there, too. If Jonathan gets overly silly and bouncy, I have a tendency to get stiff and rigid! And when I get stiff and rigid, he tends to get even more animated and buoyant in an effort to try to get me to lighten up. We actually have learned that we repel each other energetically when we are not being our true selves. The bottom line is, it doesn't work, and we either get in a fight or just remove ourselves from each other, each with a lot of judgment of how annoying the other person is being.

It just doesn't work to try to be someone you are not. If you are one of those people who does not like your Energy Type, and you related to some of the stories in this book, my guess is that you have not felt safe to live your true nature.

Here are my suggestions to help you come into your own and love it, just like the people who shared their stories for this book:

1. Give yourself some time to get acquainted with your true Energy Type. It will naturally work itself out within your own being.

2. Feel what you are feeling. You are just claiming your emotional power back from where you hid it in your childhood.

3. You liked yourself when you were a kid. You were okay with being you. Any judgment you have acquired in your life did not originate with you. It was acquired along the way to protect yourself, and you did what everyone does. You

believed it! So when you say, "I don't like my Energy Type," you are simply living in the stuff you did not believe when you were young and innocent. Then, you just went around being you. Most likely, you have parents who have different Energy Types than you, and they were doing the best they knew how to get you to be like them. You took on a lot of judgment based on other people's opinions of who they thought you should be.

4. Your internal opposition is perfect! Aren't you glad this is coming up for you? Do you really want to continue to live your life as a lie? I have learned to trust the process of life and follow where it takes me. The timing is perfect for you to know who you are and live it. Let it happen.

5. Trust me, you really do love yourself. It is impossible for you to feel anything but amazing love for the being that you are. You have just created a remarkable illusion as part of your human experience—to believe the opposite of what is really true. The truth is, we love ourselves and we can only love ourselves. The opposite illusion is that we are unacceptable, unlovable, inadequate, and not good enough. We have created this belief, and we buy into it so beautifully and fully. We have done a remarkable job of convincing ourselves this is true when it is not. I teach in my book Remembering Wholeness that if these lies were true, you would feel absolutely amazing about yourself, having discovered this truth that is actually an illusion. The fact that you feel so lousy about what you believe about yourself is the biggest red flag that you are believing a lie.

6. If you need more help with this issue, I highly recommend my best-selling book, *Remembering Wholeness: A Personal Guide to Thriving in the 21st Century*. It has helped thousands and thousands of people claim their truth and it can help you as well.

If it feels like you don't like your dominant Energy Type, that is just what you are feeling! Go ahead and feel it. Dive right into the feelings, feel them as big as they are and tell the truth about them. While you are feeling the lie, say to yourself, "What I am feeling is not true, but I have convinced myself that it is. I have fooled myself into believing that I don't like myself. The real truth is that I love myself. That is what is true. I claim my truth now. I express Type _____ Eneregy, and I love it." How many times do you need to do this? As many times as you feel the discomfort of being the true you.

I congratulate you for stepping into your truth. I congratulate you for feeling whatever is there. I want you to have your own Energy Profiling story of success and wonder. Please share it with me. I would love to hear from you and share your success with others. Just email me at carol@caroltuttle.com.

PART

- Having Fun with the Energy Profiling System

- The Four Energy Types Go to Hollywood

- The Four Energy Types Get Elected

- The Four Energy Types Date and Get Married

- The Four Energy Types Become Parents

- The Four Energy Types Get in Shape

- The Four Energy Types Get a Job

- The Four Energy Types Create a Business

- The Four Energy Types Get Dressed

Having Fun with the Energy Profiling System

ONCE YOU LEARN THE ENERGY PROFILING SYSTEM, you may have a tendency to overlay it on everything in your life. The movement of the four Energy Types can be found everywhere and in everything. Remember, they depict the four states of matter, which compose all of our human experience in the physical world—gas, liquid, plasma, and solid. Everything on this planet is created from the same four elements—nitrogen, oxygen, hydrogen, and carbon. So it is no surprise that you can relate the movement of the four Energy Types to everything you experience.

The following sections are just some examples of how my family and I have had a lot of fun using this model to better understand the world we play in. Each of these sections could be their own book!

While some of the sections are just for fun, pay special attention to the two on relationships and parenting. Using the Energy Profiling model in your relationships and in parenting will completely change your life. I mean that. More than any other resource I have implemented in my relationships and parenting, the Energy Profiling system has completely changed my own life. My marriage has experienced a complete turnaround from one of struggle and misunderstanding to one of friendship, respect, honor and great intimacy—and that after 30 years of marriage! My experience as a mother has been revolutionized. Knowing the natural tendencies of my children has allowed me to have a deep rapport and understanding of what makes them tick.

So many unnecessary judgments have gone out the window, gone for good. Enjoy this section as I introduce you to the fun of the Energy Profiling system.

The Four Types Go to Hollywood

THE FOLLOWING EXPLAINS WHY some celebrity relationships don't make it, why some movies make it big and others don't, why Simon Cowell will never understand Paula Abdul (unless he reads this book!), and why Katie Couric should have stayed on the Today Show. The Energy Profiling system adds a fun and interesting take on the events and happenings of all that is Hollywood.

THE ENERGY PROFILING SYSTEM AND AMERICAN IDOL

Let's have some fun with *American Idol*. *American Idol* is a very popular television show airing on the Fox television network. Paula Abdul, Randy Jackson, Simon Cowell, and Kara DioGuardi are the judges, each of which typifies a nearly textbook example of the four Energy Types that are expressed in people.

Paula expresses classic TYPE 1ᔆᴹ Energy. She wants everybody to win. Her comments as a judge are always about how great they did, how they look wonderful, how they should never give up, and that they can make it in their career. She is the consummate cheerleader, emitting a message of, "You can do it!" and "Believe in yourself."

Everyone loves Paula and her positive attitude, yet at the same time her quality of lightness and youthfulness makes her the judge that is taken the least seriously.

Paula also frequently tells contestants, "That was the best performance ever!" There are a lot of best performances in Paula's TYPE

1^{SM} world, because whatever is happening in the moment represents the best. People with dominant TYPE 1^{SM} Energy do not connect their past to the present, and they are not big planners on the future. If they plan for the future, there is a very good chance those plans will change. My son Mario (TYPE 1^{SM} Energy) will go see a movie and declare, "That was the best movie I've ever seen." This happens with a lot of movies. My other son Chris (TYPE 2^{SM} Energy) figures he can't take Mario's movie critique seriously, since, from his TYPE 2^{SM} perspective, there can only be one best movie you have ever seen.

Paula's physical features reflect her TYPE 1^{SM} movement in her apple cheeks, her turned-up button nose, and her buoyant movement. She is the only judge who ever gets up and dances during a performance of one of the contestants.

Randy Jackson expresses dominant TYPE 2^{SM} Energy and secondary TYPE 3^{SM} Energy. He is the nice guy of the group who attempts to throw in some edginess once in a while, but typically falls back into the nice-guy role. He notices details in the contestant's performance, attempts to share his opinion in a rougher tone, but usually ends up conveying his thoughts with a soft-spoken nature. Randy's physical features reflect his TYPE 2^{SM} movement in his softened, blended facial features. His bone structure throughout his body is all softened corners.

Kara DioGuardi, the new judge on the block as of 2009, is a dominant TYPE 3^{SM} Energy. Simon Fuller—creator and executive producer of *American Idol*—describes Kara's TYPE 3^{SM} Energy perfectly: "We are turning the heat up on *Idol* this year and are thrilled to welcome Kara to the judges' table. She is a smart, sassy lady, and one of America's most successful songwriters." Kara describes herself as feisty and unpredictable. Kara's physical features reflect her TYPE 3^{SM} movement with her deeper smile lines, lump of clay nose and exotic, angled eyes. Her bone structure is more angled and chiseled.

Then there is Simon Cowell. There couldn't be a more perfect example of a TYPE 4^{SM} Energy! You always know where Simon stands and what he really thinks about each performance. He says it like it is. In his mind, the show clearly is a competition, and if you're bad, you're bad! His black-and-white thought process and keen ability to notice any flaws allow him to quickly assess a performance and give authoritative feedback to the contestant. Even though the audience boos and hisses him, they turn to Simon as the authority who determines the best performances. Simon is very bold and clear in his assessment. In his mind, it is a singing competition and that is how he treats it. Simon's square facial features, nearly straight eyebrows, dark coloring, and striking looks tip us off as to what Energy Type he is. And the way people react to Simon helps us, too. Many are openly offended by Simon's self-assurance about what is correct. However, they usually come around to see that he is not really being mean, only honest about his convictions and both clear and precise in expressing them.

He also has a typical TYPE 4^{SM} response to Paula's TYPE 1^{SM} enthusiasm: that she is silly and doesn't know what she is talking about. Paula's TYPE 1^{SM} priority is making sure the contestant feels good about themselves—she uplifts them. Simon's priority is telling the truth as he sees it and perfecting the contestant's performance by pointing out their flaws.

One of my favorite episodes was when a viewer called in to talk to Simon. Her question for Simon was, "Why do you apologize every time you give the contestants critical feedback?" Simon answered with a classic TYPE 4^{SM} response: "I like you, I don't know, I am not going to do that anymore!" And I am sure he hasn't!

THE ENERGY PROFILING SYSTEM IN HOLLYWOOD

When Hollywood casts the right person in the right movie, it can be a huge success. Some of the best examples are found in the following movies:

- TYPE 1^{SM} Energy: One of the most classic examples of a TYPE 1^{SM} movie that cast a TYPE 1^{SM} actress was *Legally Blonde* with Reese Witherspoon. Reese Witherspoon is a dominant TYPE 1^{SM} actress playing a TYPE 1^{SM} character in a totally exaggerated TYPE 1^{SM} movie. It is about a young co-ed who follows her ex-boyfriend to law school to win him back. No one takes her seriously, but through the entire movie, she proves everyone wrong as she lives in her random, buoyant, light nature.

- TYPE 2^{SM} Energy: Any romance and romantic comedy that casts a TYPE 2^{SM} male actor will do well. TYPE 2^{SM} men are heart-centered, subtle, soft, and romantic. Richard Gere in *Pretty Woman* is a perfect example. Both Julia Roberts and Richard Gere express dominant TYPE 2^{SM} Energy. They easily portrayed connection, heart, romance, and sensitivity in this big Hollywood hit.

- TYPE 3^{SM} Energy: Harrison Ford in the *Indiana Jones* series expresses all TYPE 3^{SM} Energy. Harrison Ford played a dominant TYPE 3^{SM} character in a story line that is all bigger-than-life, risk, and adventure made this a sure Hollywood hit.

- TYPE 4^{SM} Energy: *The Matrix* is a TYPE 4^{SM} movie with a thought-provoking storyline. All three major leads— Keeanu Reeves, Laurence Fishburne, and Carrie-Anne Moss—express dominant TYPE 4^{SM} Energy.

A good example of a movie not standing out due to a miscast is TYPE 4^{SM} Keeanu Reeves in the TYPE 2^{SM} romantic film *The Lakehouse*. A romantic film that casts a TYPE 4^{SM} actor as a lead will never win our hearts over. Just like Keeanu Reeves in *The Lakehouse*, a TYPE 4^{SM} lead will come across too stiff and rigid in a movie that is trying to depict a soft, subtle, heartfelt character.

THE ENERGY PROFILING SYSTEM IN THE NEWS

When Katie Couric—who expresses dominant TYPE 1^{SM} Energy—left the fun, light, chatty anchor spot on the Today Show for the hardliner, serious, single anchor of the CBS Evening News, the ratings began to dive to record lows. She had a hard time convincing her viewing public and critics that she could pull it off. Following Dan Rather (who expresses dominant TYPE 4^{SM} Energy), and trying to portray a presence and image that is not her true nature cannot convince anyone. We just know something is not right. What is not right is that we can never completely camouflage our natural gifts and talents to try and portray something we are not. Katie looks very lonely sitting by herself, sharing all the awful things that are happening in the world. It is just not right for her! This is just another example of a person with TYPE 1^{SM} Energy thinking they have to go against their true nature to be taken seriously.

THE ENERGY PROFILING SYSTEM AND HOLLYWOOD MARRIAGES

When Tom Cruise and Nicole Kidman's marriage didn't make it and they went their separate ways, consider the possibility that their dominant Energy Types may have had something to do with it. With Tom expressing dominant TYPE 4^{SM} Energy and and Nicole Nicole expressing dominant TYPE 3^{SM} Energy, and both being Hollywood superstars, there is the potential for a lot of struggle between such intense, bold energies. After the divorce, Tom married Katie Holmes who expresses dominant TYPE 1^{SM} Energy and Nicole married Keith Urban who expresses dominant TYPE 2^{SM} Energy—both lighter energies. Katie's adaptable nature adapted so much to Tom's structure that she divorced him to experience her light, free energy again. Keith Urban appears to have succeeded in not blending into the background next to Nicole's fiery nature, maintaining his own happiness, which is a core need in any marriage.

THE ENERGY PROFILING SYSTEM AND
RACHAEL RAY'S SUCCESS

The Rachael Ray show is a huge success. Rachael Ray expresses a dominant TYPE 1^{SM} Energy. At a time when there is so much talk about economic uncertainty, terrorism, challenges in families and personal lives, the public looks to be uplifted and laugh over things that are not too deep, eager to add more light and fun to their lives. Rachael Ray is the gal that brings that to us every day of the week with her buoyant, radiant nature. Her animation is not an act. Her enthusiasm is legitimate. She truly loves her job and loves putting a smile on your face.

At the same time she has hit the big leagues and is a network success, a series of "I Hate Rachael Ray" websites cropped up. I thought this was very curious and began to investigate. It won't surprise you that one of the most popular I found had a picture of the creator of the website, a woman who expresses dominant TYPE 4^{SM} Energy! Her comments include, "Rachael Ray is annoying for many reasons but here are a few: she is repetitive, she talks with her hands way too much, she giggles incessantly."

Personally, I am fine with Rachael Ray. I love the fact that she is living her truth and sharing her natural gifts and talents.

My hope for the Energy Profiling system is that it will help people recognize the deep, driving force our energy has on us, that is creating in us and influencing the expression of who we are. I hope we learn to drop the judgments that are so unnecessary in a world that would be incredibly boring if we were all the same!

The Four Types Get Elected

WATCHING PRESIDENTIAL CAMPAIGNS THROUGH the lens of the four Energy Types is a blast! Regardless of what you think of the parties or the issues, watching the candidates move through the experience (true to their nature or not) is so interesting.

Here is a rundown of the primary candidates' Energy Types during the United States' 2008 presidential election, including a spouse.

On the Democratic ticket:
1. President Barack Obama—Dominant TYPE 3^{SM} Energy with secondary TYPE 4^{SM} Energy
2. Vice President Joe Biden—Dominant TYPE 3^{SM} Energy with secondary TYPE 4^{SM} Energy
3. First Lady Michelle Obama—Dominant TYPE 3^{SM} Energy with secondary TYPE 1^{SM} Energy

On the Republican side:
1. John McCain—Dominant TYPE 4^{SM} Energy with secondary TYPE 2^{SM} Energy
2. Sarah Palin—Dominant TYPE 1^{SM} Energy with a secondary TYPE 4^{SM} Energy

I'll begin by saying here that I do not mean to imply any favor towards any candidate or party. Any observations I make are strictly in terms of the Energy Profiling system, not in terms of advocacy or detraction.

John McCain's TYPE 4^{SM} nature came out in his reputation for being a hero, a loyal citizen who served his country in the military. He was seen by many as an authority and a bold leader. However, he did not exude warmth and dynamism due to his more cool, structured nature. Even his war injuries cause his body to have a more rigid movement.

Sarah Palin seemed appealing at first, but was later completely misunderstood, especially by the media. She truly lived up to her TYPE 1^{SM} nature by being animated, random, perky, and uplifting. But she was dressed in TYPE 4^{SM} design elements in an effort to make her look more serious and business-like, which undermined her natural gifts. When her animation came pouring out, it unfortunately came across a lot more amplified and the media had a heyday making fun of her.

With his dominant TYPE 3^{SM} Energy, President Obama won people over naturally with his dynamic confidence and willingness to take on a tough job at a tough time, and turn things around. He truly depicts a character that will judge his own effectiveness by his results. You can be sure that making a lasting impression as a president is what drives him, as well as getting the kind of results that help more Americans. His secondary TYPE 4^{SM} Energy comes out in his clear, bold speech and his concise ability to articulate himself. If, like George H.W. Bush, he takes his TYPE 3^{SM} Energy to the extreme without keeping balance with other energies, it is possible that Obama could isolate himself from his constituents and the rest of the world. Joe Biden and the First Lady Michelle Obama also express dominant TYPE 3^{SM} Energy, and we , and we can expect them to focus on getting the job done and making a difference.

In 2012, President Obama ran for office again. The run-up to the Republican nomination was interesting to watch as candidates of varying Energy Types tried to grab the spotlight. Candidates represented a lot of TYPE 3^{SM} and TYPE 4^{SM} Energy on the debate stages.

Only one TYPE 1^{SM} candidate joined the race—Ron Paul—and we didn't see any TYPE 2^{SM} candidates in the running that year. They were probably planning all the details that went into the campaigns!

Mitt Romney eventually secured the nomination and ran against President Obama. All throughout Romney's campaign, he faced the challenge of being called stiff, robotic, or distant. Because he expresses strong dominant TYPE 4^{SM} Energy, he might come across that way. He naturally expressed a more still, rigid movement that many perceived as unapproachable. While he exceled in more structured, presidential-looking settings such as formal debates, he experienced some gaffe situations at the informal, town-hall meetings that ran contrary to his nature by putting him on the spot.

I don't endorse any candidate or political party here. I just share this information for fun and learning's sake. Even the frenzied world of politics looks a little clearer because of the Energy Profiling system.

The Four Types Date and Get Married

FOR THE FIRST TIME, we can take a peek into the future to see which potential challenges and strengths a serious relationship such as dating or marriage will face—all as a result of knowing the combination of the two partners' Energy Types.

We frequently use the terms *type* and *chemistry* when we refer to the nature of dating and romantic relationships. For example, if you are not attracted to someone, you might say, "They are not my type!" Or, if you think two people get along really well and make a great couple, you might say, "They have great chemistry!" I find it interesting that, once again, we are using language that coincides with the Energy Profiling system as an underlying cause of what influences this dynamic. Since the four Energy Types refer to the four elements from which we are all created—nitrogen, oxygen, hydrogen, and carbon—this knowledge brings a much deeper meaning and understanding to why we use these terms!

DATING YOUR "TYPE" WITH THE ENERGY PROFILING SYSTEM

If you are currently open to dating more than one person, the Energy Profiling model can help you zero in on who you are most interested in, and know the reason why. Consider the kind of relationship you want to create, consider how your own Energy Type will contribute to that dynamic, and what Energy Type of potential partner would be most supportive for you to find.

- A TYPE 1^{SM} partner will naturally bring a lot of fun and lightness to a relationship. Dating them can feel like uplifting and invigorating. They tend to always have an idea of something new to do together. As they are socially oriented to their life experiences, expect them to be connected (then disconnected, then connected again) with many varied people and to bring you into that experience.

- A TYPE 2^{SM} partner will really connect at the heart. Regardless of being male or female, they will be more oriented to talking about feelings and connecting in a one-on-one experience. They tend to notice details about their partners and use those details to plan thoughtful gestures. They bring a calming quality to their dating relationships.

- A TYPE 3^{SM} partner will infuse a relationship with passion and activity. They tend to know very quickly whether or not they want to pursue a relationship further. Their natural gift for motivating and encouraging others will give a forward, active push to the things you do together.

- A TYPE 4^{SM} partner will add structure to a relationship. Although people with TYPE 4^{SM} Energy don't express their feelings readily to everyone, they feel deeply, and if they are committed to you, they remain deeply loyal. They give 100% to a relationship in which they feel respected. Because they view the world through an analytical lens, they often initiate conversations about ideas over those about feelings.

My third child and second daughter, Anne, was my first child to use the Energy Profiling system as a reference tool in her dating relationships and marriage decision. (My two older children had already met and married their spouses prior to this information being developed enough to be useful to them at that time in their lives.)

After dating every Energy Type of guy, it became more and more clear to Anne that the qualities she was most drawn to and well matched for were found in a TYPE 3^{SM} companion. Interestingly enough, she came to meet her future husband through an Energy Profiling/Dressing Your Truth event.

At that time, we regularly offered Energy Profiling and Dressing Your Truth events at the world-renowned Red Mountain Spa in the spectacular setting of Southern Utah. At the opening dinner of such an event, Anne introduced herself and shared with our group that she was single and was open to being set up with someone. Attending this event was a mother with her two grown daughters. After Anne shared this, they all looked at each other with big eyes and agreed they needed to introduce their son and brother Tanner to Anne.

Before the week had ended, we had seen pictures of Tanner and heard a lot about his nature. Anne and I were pretty confident he expressed dominant TYPE 3^{SM} Energy. Tanner's TYPE 3^{SM} sister Anna, who was at the event, took the lead to make things happen and make sure they met. They went on their first date in late July 2008, and were happily married in late January 2009. They fit like a hand and glove with each other. Their natural tendencies complement each other so well. I am so happy to have my new son-in-law Tanner (TYPE 3^{SM} Energy) and my daughter-in-law Sarah (TYPE 3^{SM} Energy) join our family. I am no longer the lonely TYPE 3^{SM} family member! It is good to have some more dynamic, sure, swift company in the family.

MAKING YOUR MARRIAGE AMAZING

I married my own husband long before I knew about the Energy Profiling information. As I mentioned before, discovering our Energy Types opened us up to a relationship of less judgment and more joy. If you are married, learning your Energy Type and your spouse's Energy Type can do the very same thing for you. By understanding the natural movement that you both express, you can create a marriage that is more supportive for you both.

Every combination of Energy Types experiences its unique strengths and challenges. Whichever dominant Energy Types you and your spouse express, two important things will maximize the strengths and minimize the challenges:

1. Live true to your nature. Dysfunction occurs in our relationships when we think we must live contrary to our true natures in order to be loved. If you are trying to conform to a set of expectations about what you *should* be in your marriage, stop. Consider the possibility that your core, true self is already lovable. The good news is, when you live true to your nature, you naturally invite others to do the same. You can't change the way your partner acts, only yourself. But when you act in alignment with your best self, limiting patterns in your relationship naturally shift along with you.

2. Honor your partner in living true to their nature. You and your spouse both need space, time, and permission to just be yourselves. What that looks like for your spouse will be different than it is for you. In this book, you've learned what each Energy Type needs and prioritizes, so make sure you offer that gift to your spouse. Stop trying to make your spouse conform to your wishes and just allow them to be. You may find that doing so gives them the freedom and respect they've needed to become even better than you ever expected.

For more specific tips for your particular relationship, visit The Carol Blog. We've covered the strengths and challenges of all 10 possible combinations of Energy Types in relationships. You'll find this information in the Relationships Guide at thecarolblog.com.

The Four Types Become Parents

USING THE ENERGY PROFILING SYSTEM AS A GUIDE to understanding your children's true nature and how to best support them as a parent is a gift I wish I'd had when my children were little. I truly believe it is never too late to be a good parent, so I am grateful I have it now to support my adult children. I am having fun using it with my grandchildren and supporting my own children in using it as parents.

In October 2012, I published *The Child Whisperer*. This book applies the Energy Profiling system to children and outlines an intuitive parenting approach that supports children in being happier, successful, and more cooperative. I am grateful that thousands of parents have embraced this style of parenting that really honors their children. Imagine what a better world we could live in if an entire generation of children grew up understanding their true natures and living true to the highest version of themselves!

OUR ENERGY TYPE FROM BIRTH

While personality develops over time, our core movement and vibration are with us from birth. You expressed your Energy Type in the womb! Because this system is based on assessing movement and not personality, you can understand and honor a child's true nature from their earliest days.

I was sensitive enough to let my daughter Jenny (TYPE 1^{SM} Energy) lead in the conversation of what she thought Seth's dominant Energy

Type was when he was first born. I did not bring it up until she led the conversation in that direction. When Seth was three months old, the topic came up naturally, and I asked her what she thought his Energy Type was. I had already come to the conclusion that he expressed dominant TYPE 4^{SM} Energy, as my daughter Anne and daughter-in-law Sarah thought as well. Jenny exclaimed, "Oh, he expresses TYPE 4^{SM} Energy." I got very excited and said, "That is exactly what I think!" I asked her how long she had sensed this, and she said that even from the first week of his life she could feel it in him. Now, a baby does not usually display their dominant personality or even body features when they are a week old, but Jenny could feel Seth's vibration. She knows the Energy Profiling system, and she knew he expressed TYPE 4^{SM} Energy within days of his birth. Could you imagine the difference it would make in this world if every parent could identify their baby's Energy Type shortly after birth?

Because of what Jenny knows, she has been able to parent him in a way that supports his true nature. For example, Jenny knows Seth prefers spending some time by himself. She regularly does not go get him out of his crib for about 10 minutes after he wakes up from a nap to give him that chance to be by himself. He is perfectly content with this.

Jenny is a gifted vocalist and a talented actress. She regularly loves to dance and sing at home, being true to her TYPE 1^{SM} nature. She has come to learn that Seth has more fun sitting, watching, and giggling at his mom than being picked up and danced around with her.

Seth likes to use his gift for intense focusing on anything he can. On a recent family trip to Hawaii, he spent nearly an hour on the beach finding small rocks and placing them together to form a straight line.

We have been dressing Seth in his truth from his infancy. I have to say he one of the best-dressed babies around! While most people refer to babies as cute, with Seth's dressed in his TYPE 4^{SM} clothes, people always say what a handsome baby he is. Jenny even heard a little girl at church comment one Sunday, "Mom, that baby is going to be really handsome when he grows up!"

Since the first printing of this book, more grandchildren have joined our family: Jenny's two sons, Joseph (TYPE 3^{SM} Energy) and Neal (TYPE 2^{SM} Energy), and also Anne's daughter Katie Claire (TYPE 3^{SM} Energy). These children moved with a distinct energy from their very first day. As they have honored their children's true natures, both Jenny and Anne and their spouses have created a parenting experience that is free from the struggles that many parents experience.

THE FOUR TYPES OF CHILDREN

Every child is unique, and knowing their distinct Type of energy will help you know how to parent them uniquely. The Fun-loving TYPE 1^{SM} Child connects to the world socially and needs space to create fun. The Sensitive TYPE 2^{SM} Child relates to the world emotionally and prioritizes having their feelings heard. The Determined TYPE 3^{SM} Child approaches the world physically and needs the opportunity for new challenges. The More Serious TYPE 4^{SM} Child views the world intellectually and their primary need is to be respected.

Look for the dominant Energy Types in your own children, grandchildren, or just the other children around you, and honor them accordingly. Gently help parents of children to understand their children's Energy Types and watch how harmonious their relationships become as the parent no longer forces the child in a direction that is not true to his or her Energy Type.

(For more information about how to parent a child true to his or her nature, see the Additional Resource section in this book.)

THE FOUR TYPES GET IN SHAPE

KNOWING OUR DOMINANT ENRGY TYPE can make a difference in knowing how to better support ourselves in staying physically fit.

Consider the possibility that the earlier approaches you have attempted have failed because they go against the natural design of who you are. People too often think every approach to diet and fitness should work for all people. This is absolutely not true. With the help of knowing our dominant Energy Type, we can more beautifully craft a life that supports us in all areas by living true to who we are individually. It is beneficial to create a fitness plan that matches your natural movement.

- TYPE 1^{SM} Energy: You are best supported by crisp, fresh foods and social opportunities to exercise. Just talking to my daughter Jenny (TYPE 1^{SM} Energy) about how her buoyant, random movement affects her exercise and diet routine, I learned that she prefers to try a variety of fitness and recreational activities and be just good enough in them to enjoy them. She enjoys variety in her food and finds it hard to stick to an eating plan 100 percent without making some changes to it along the way.

- A TYPE 2^{SM} Energy: You are the most sensitive to food and physical activities. This does not mean you are weaker—it just means that you have a higher awareness and response to physical input that affects you. You are best supported by eating blended foods with textures that feel comfortable, and by a detailed plan for exercise. You get better results with steady, consistent activity as opposed to spurts of high-intensity activity.

- A TYPE 3^{SM} Energy: You best achieve your fitness goals by eating foods with more substance to them, by switching up your exercise routine, and having an end result in mind. If it's a result brought about by an event or competition, all the better. When I was training for marathons, running became a means to an end result, which made it much more likely for me to want to do it. Exercise is a place where TYPE 3^{SM} Energy is really allowed to go big physically, which is very supportive to staying in alignment with your true nature.

- A TYPE 4^{SM} Energy: You are best supported by consistency, both in meals and exercise. You may prefer little variety in their diet, eating the same thing for a certain meal for years. For example, Jenny's husband Tony (TYPE 4^{SM} Energy) has a preferred lunch of a turkey sandwich with cheese and lettuce, some lemon sandwich cookies, a pudding cup, and a piece of fruit. This has been his pattern for over 20 years! He has been eating the same lunch nearly every day since he was in grade school.

  I noticed the same thing with my son's girlfriend (TYPE 4^{SM} Energy), when we spent a week together in New York City. Nearly every night, she ordered some variety of pasta. When we got home she shared with Mario, "I really ventured out and tried some new things when we ate out." I said to her "You had pasta every night, it was the same thing!" She explained to me, "No, I usually order the same kind of pasta, but this time I tried some new varieties."

  Due to your all-or-nothing nature, you will either exercise diligently or not at all. If you express dominant TYPE 4^{SM} Energy and you don't exercise at all, a change just requires you making a commitment. If you say you will do something, you will.

THE FOUR TYPES GET A JOB

ANOTHER HUGE AREA IN LIFE where the Energy Profiling system can sort a lot of things out is the job market. Imagine a dominant TYPE 1ˢᴹ person trying to be an accountant! Or a dominant TYPE 2ˢᴹ person in sales that requires contacting leads through cold calling to get them to buy your service or product. How about a dominant TYPE 3ˢᴹ person working for a dominant TYPE 2ˢᴹ who wants a lot of details and thinks the TYPE 3ˢᴹ person is taking too many risks?

SEEING YOUR WORKPLACE THROUGH NEW EYES

At a past Dressing Your Truth men's event, one of our attendees—who expresses dominant TYPE 3ˢᴹ Energy—shared, "Now I know why I am so frustrated at my job. I have a TYPE 2ˢᴹ boss who approaches things so differently than me. I have not been given the liberty to do my job my way, and it is driving me nuts. I felt frustrated that he is always checking on me for details that I didn't feel mattered. It all makes sense now. I know I won't change him, so I think I will change jobs where I can really let my natural gifts and talents make a difference!"

I could go on and on about the scenarios that are doomed for frustration and potential failure when it comes to the line of work we choose that is not a match for our true nature.

"Recently I was shopping for life insurance online. I knew what insurance company I wanted, and I found a local agency that represented that company. I am a TYPE 2^{SM} *[person], so I, of course, wanted to be comfortable with the salesperson I worked with. Fortunately, the local agency had pictures of all their partners and sales staff on their website. I just looked at all the pictures until I found a TYPE 2*^{SM} *[salesperson], and then gave him a call!*

"My agent turned out to be very easy to work with—for me. He communicated clearly, and signing up for my new policy was a snap. The Energy Profiling system helps me know what to expect from others, and lets me move forward—even with strangers— with a great deal of confidence."

—MIKE FITZGERALD (TYPE 2^{SM} ENERGY), UTAH

The world has changed. We are no longer inclined to stick it out in our jobs like our parents did. The rule of thumb in our parents' time was, "You get a job and stay with it your entire lifetime." It's pretty clear that this is no longer the employee mentality! If you are not happy and feeling fulfilled, you go out and find another job or profession. Not knowing their own natural tendencies and gifts and talents may have something to do with the rate at which people change jobs and careers. Think how much easier it will be now that you know your Energy Type.

Currently the academic, corporate, and much of the working world has been referring to the Myers-Briggs profiling system to help you and companies identify where you best fit in the working world. I remember taking these tests, but the results were so impractical to me that I paid no attention to them. Obviously, I never even thought about it again when it came to the choices I made in creating my profession.

HOW TO CHOOSE THE RIGHT JOB FOR YOUR ENERGY TYPE

I really believe that you can be successful in any career. But you need the freedom to move through it true to your natural movement. Before you accept your next job offer, or decide to stick it out in the job you're in now, consider a few necessities specific to your Energy Type:

- TYPE 1^{SM} Energy: You thrive in positions with flexibility in your schedule, varied social interactions, and opportunities to share your ideas in a fun way.

- TYPE 2^{SM} Energy: You do best in positions that allow you to complete tasks at your own pace, connect with others comfortably, and optimize your gift for detail-oriented planning.

- TYPE 3^{SM} Energy: You work best in high-pressure situations that require swift thinking. You enjoy the opportunity to take charge, motivate others, and accomplish multiple tasks simultaneously.

- TYPE 4^{SM} Energy: You need a work environment where you feel respected and are seen as an authority. You work most efficiently in a position with systems that you can give feedback on to improve.

I look forward to continuing our work with individuals and companies to help them better understand their most valuable asset: their employees. We have already had the opportunity to assist companies in bringing their employees through an Energy Profiling class, as the following story from Sheryl Laukat attests.

"All of the employees at our local facility took Carol's Energy Profiling classes. How has it helped? Two basic ways:

"First—A greater appreciation for each other. We learned that each one of us has strengths we bring to the table. Our eyes opened up as to why we don't all see things the same. No one has to be like anyone else, even within the same energy. However, general strengths are often easy to spot.

"For example, we have three long-time employees who happen to be artists in their spare time. We recently asked them to help make our company unique by learning the art of hand-engraving our saxophones. This is nearly a lost art and requires a lot of patience, detailed skill, and flexibility with wrist movement. The hand engraving is magnificent and exquisite, and it is interesting to note that each of the employees who do the engraving has a dominant TYPE 2SM Energy.

"Other examples:

"In our company, we easily know who can lighten a tense moment with customers and employees (often those with dominant TYPE 1SM Energy).

"Some see the big forest of how what we do today will affect us in 20 years (often TYPE 4SM Energy).

"I hired an assistant who has TYPE 2SM qualities because I am weak at details. She catches my mistakes. Because of what I learned with Carol, I knew what I was looking for when interviewing possible candidates for that position.

"Our company has been able to accomplish a great deal in a short time. Now we know why—we have more TYPE 3SM employees than anything else. And we've noted that several of our employees have TYPE 3SM Energy as a secondary energy, even if it isn't their dominant.

"We consider our company to be innovative and creative. We come up with a lot of ideas, often offered by employees with TYPE 1^{SM} Energy (dominant or secondary).

"It is very important to note we all had to learn and acknowledge that we are not stuck in a category. However, knowing our nature is the absolute basis of building on our strengths and improving our weaknesses. Grasping that concept has allowed us to accept each other and ourselves for what we have to offer while not closing the door for any of our possibilities.

"Second—Better communication and understanding. One employee might say to another, 'I understand that the TYPE 3^{SM} Energy in you wants to get this done ASAP, but I hope we can take time to make sure it's as good as possible.' There is an instant understanding between the two employees, without causing an argument. They look at both sides—the project needs to get done quickly, and it needs to be done correctly.

"Or someone might say, 'The TYPE 4^{SM} Energy in me is requesting that the address labels are straight.' That statement is not comprehended as being critical; it's just the way a TYPE 4^{SM} Energy sees things.

"Sometimes I ask a certain employee with a TYPE 1^{SM} Energy to look at my email before I send it. He might say, 'Hmm. The direct, strong approach with that particular customer might cause some misunderstandings.' I'll listen to the suggestion.

"In the past, some employees were hurt by other employees blunt statements or actions. As the boss, I was often spending time trying to repair the situations (some caused by me). We need a lot less fixing now! We still have some problems, but we understand each other better and have become more sensitive and forgiving on both sides.

"The office atmosphere has definitely improved because of our increased perception. We've had moments with positive laughter from 'getting it' about ourselves and others, and we've also had some retrospective Ah-ha moments. I can't imagine our workplace functioning as well as it does now without using our knowledge of the Energy Profiling system."

— SHERYL LAUKAT (TYPE 4^{SM} ENERGY),
CANNONBALL MUSICAL INSTRUMENTS, UTAH

THE FOUR TYPES CREATE A BUSINESS

BUSINESS OWNERS OFTEN CREATE A BUSINESS that reflects their own dominant Energy Type, or an Energy Type that wisely matches with the product or service they offer. Some of the best examples are found in the following restaurants and retail businesses.

Jack in the Box is a fast food chain and is definitely a TYPE 1^{SM} restaurant. All the way from its branding—complete with a clown—to its menu. The menu has so many choices that the restaurant can't decide if it wants to be a hamburger, Mexican, or Asian fast food chain. At the other end of the spectrum, you have In-and-Out Burger, which is a very TYPE 4^{SM} restaurant. The design lines of the restaurant, the menu, and the customer focus all reflect TYPE 4^{SM} Energy. They have the smallest, most precise menu of any fast food chain I know. They only offer a few items on the menu: hamburgers, fries, and drinks. That's it. Their focus is to be perfect in what they deliver. They have been able to duplicate their success in every location they have opened.

In the women's retail fashion world, we have found that certain stores consistently sell clothing that express one of the four Energy Types, according to our Dressing Your Truth system.

You can find a lot of TYPE 1^{SM} clothes at the Gap. J. Jill is almost completely a TYPE 2^{SM} clothing store. Chico's and Coldwater Creek do the best in creating TYPE 3^{SM} clothing, and Talbots and Express carry predominantly TYPE 4^{SM} clothes.

HOW TO START A BUSINESS TRUE TO YOUR TYPE

While reading about the four Energy Types, you may have noticed that I described those with TYPE 3^{SM} Energy as natural entrepreneurs. While they do have a natural knack for getting a business up and running, every Energy Type can be a successful entrepreneur if they approach the experience true to their nature.

- TYPE 1^{SM} Energy: Your gift for ideas gives you a real edge in coming up with a great business concept. Your natural tendency toward optimism inspires others with hope that your business idea can become a reality. Your challenge is follow-through, so surround yourself with people who can finish up projects when you need to move to the next new thing.

- TYPE 2^{SM} Energy: When you start a business, you naturally collect loads of information and make detailed plans. These plans can support you in finding the best resources and deciding on the best way to move forward. Your challenge is getting stuck in the planning phase, so decide the day on which you'll say, "My plan is good enough," and just move forward on making your plans a reality.

- TYPE 3^{SM} Energy: As I said, if you express dominant TYPE 3^{SM} Energy, you have a natural tendency toward entrepreneurship. This is because your results-oriented nature sees money as a result. Your challenge is jumping in too quickly without necessary details, or starting so many projects that you burn out or lose interest. Draw on your secondary Energy Types to support you in managing those challenges.

- TYPE 4^{SM} Energy: You are good at working well on your own—an important gift for an entrepreneur. You also excel at fixing flawed systems, so taking over for a business that's struggling may actually be a better fit than starting a business from scratch. Your challenge is delegation because you see the best way to do things. Decide on what *must* be perfect and give your support team more freedom to accomplish the other tasks in their own way.

The Four Types Get Dressed

NOW THAT YOU'VE SEEN how many ways your Energy Type affects your life, consider with me the one area of your life that's affected daily that you might not have even realized: getting dressed. You move through life in a unique way. It's honoring of your Energy Type to make sure that the movement you wear on your body also matches the movement of your true nature. It makes a huge difference that most people are not even aware of.

Consider the possibility that every day you are putting on clothing whose movement conflicts with the ability to express the core, true nature of who you are. The current fashion trends attempt to teach us how to put on style or beauty. But the online courses I've created teach you how to put the right movement on your body to bring out your natural beauty and good looks.

WHY DRESSING TRUE TO YOUR TYPE MATTERS

When you discover your Energy Type, you know you inner strengths and gifts better than you ever have before—you know what you are able to share with the world. But that doesn't mean that people you meet will naturally understand and relate to you. When you put a style on your body that outwardly expresses your true nature, you help other people to instantly and intuitively recognize you for who you are. It's almost like others know what to expect from you and so they respond to you more positively than they would if your inner and outer expressions conflicted. When your inner and outer expression line up, you naturally communicate more easily, feel more confident, and experience more success. Imagine what a difference this can make in your own personal experience and interactions at work and any sort of social activity you engage in.

Both men and women face the challenge of not liking their body or struggling with their weight, on either end of the scale. When you put clothes on your body in alignment with who you are, you essentially send your body the message that it's okay to live true to your natural movement. You feel more comfortable in your own skin, and people notice that extra confidence.

Women experience the added challenge of navigating all the myths and bad advice from the fashion world that point them in the wrong direction. The fashion world wants to keep you confused so you are dependent on the latest fashion trend and you continually have to purchase new clothes to stay in style. What I have seen is that most women give up and resort to a pair of jeans and a t-shirt for their day-to-day wear, with an occasional need to fix themselves up for an outing. Those few women who are drawn to fashion are typically following fashion trends rather than their own true nature because they have not known what it is.

Consider the possibility that when you have been complimented on how you look people are noticing the article of clothing rather than noticing you. You will hear compliments like, "I really like your jacket," or, "That is a great purse." When you are Dressing Your Truth you will hear, "You look amazing," and, "Wow, what have you done? You have never looked so great." That is because with Dressing Your Truth you are expressing wholeness and your entire being is looking vibrant and handsome.

One of the biggest fashion mistakes women make is believing the fallacy that all women can wear black. Think about it. How much movement is there in the color black? Absolutely none. Black is the stillest of all colors. Now that you know the primary movement of each Energy Type, which Energy Type holds the movement of stillness?

Right, a TYPE 4^{SM}.

In our Dressing Your Truth model we teach that the only men and women who should be wearing black—and they look absolutely stunning in it—are those with a dominant TYPE 4^{SM} expression. Everyone gasps and goes into a tailspin, exclaiming, "What will I do with all my black clothes?" Give them to your TYPE 4^{SM} friend or burn them. Get over it! You will learn very quickly once you put yourself in colors that honor your true nature that black is not a color you will miss.

I used to have about 30 percent of my wardrobe in black. I have absolutely none in my closet today, and not one day since have I awakened and thought, "Boy, I miss my black clothes. I am so sad I can't wear them!"

The only reason you think you need black is because for several decades the so-called fashion experts have been telling you everyone can wear it and have been teaching that black is a neutral, slimming color that looks great on everyone. Baloney! That is not true. If you express dominant TYPE 3^{SM} Energy with some wonderful texture, deep smile and facial lines going on in your facial features, put some black on only if you want to instantly add 20 years to your appearance. If you express dominant TYPE 1^{SM} Energy and you want to confuse people to perceive you as a still, serious person, and you want your animation to be exaggerated and judged as inappropriate, wear a lot of black!

HOW DRESSING YOUR TRUE TO YOUR ENERGY TYPE WORKS

Dressing Your Truth for women and men are online video courses that give you practical tools to dress true to your nature. We teach you how to identify clothes that will coincide with and express your dominant Energy Type. In these two programs, five specific elements create the movement in your clothes and style.

They are:
1. Design Lines
2. Fabrication
3. Texture
4. Pattern
5. Color or Chroma

For men, this is pretty straightforward and applies mostly to your clothes and hairstyle. For women, makeup and jewelry are additional components to take into account.

Dressing true to your Energy Type supports you in a daily practice of affirming the truth of who you are. In our online courses, we teach men and women how to find and wear the clothes that honor your natural gifts and talents. For example, my clothes all hold the vibration of my TYPE 3/4 key words, which are dynamic, rich, textured, angled, and bold. I know the design lines, fabrication, texture, pattern, and chroma that create this movement, so I choose the clothes that match it. I am reminded daily that this is who I am. Because I am Dressing My Truth, I express my true nature in what I wear to everyone I interact with.

When you learn to Dress Your Truth, you will discover why you have always been drawn to and loved certain articles of clothing. I was always drawn to animal print, and I never knew why. Now I know! I know why certain garments in my wardrobe were my favorites. I now see that they had the correct elements that honored my Energy Type. I had unknowingly purchased what was perfect for me. We'll teach you how to tune into your style or beauty sixth sense so that you know the mechanics behind what you like so you get it right every single time.

"The Energy Profiling system and Dressing Your Truth have dramatically changed my life in a few short months. My six daughters and I read Remembering Wholeness at the beginning of 2007, which introduced us to energy work and the power we have to create the lives we want through our thoughts and intentions. What a shift it was for us!

"My daughter Karalee had a strong desire to attend a Vibrant Woman Dressing Your Truth event, which she did in October 2007. Her physical and emotional transformation, as well as her enthusiasm for her new knowledge…was contagious and we all resolved to attend.

"My opportunity came a few months later in March 2008, when I attended a Dressing Your Truth event with my sister and two of my daughters, ages 29 and 18. I was a few days away from turning 51 and feeling old and frumpy. I had never worn much makeup and had always envied women who seemed to have a natural fashion sense. How did they know what looked good on them? How did they manage that "put together" look? I had always had great hair but it was now sporting a lot of gray. I had decided to try to age gracefully, and so was avoiding coloring it, but I felt my hair was making me look older than my age. I was definitely ready for a new look!

"And a new TYPE 4^{SM} look is what I got! My before and after pictures are evidence that my transformation was dramatic. I found out that my TYPE 2^{SM} sister's gray silver streaks were perfect for her look, but mine had to go. I went home with my hair colored and cut, new makeup, the knowledge of what to look for in clothing, a newfound excitement for shopping, and a resolve to dress my truth for the 30-day challenge period. I went through my already sparse closet (I put off buying clothes because I wanted to

go down a size first!) and weeded out anything that wasn't right for me.

"When I returned home, my family, friends, and colleagues were amazed by the difference. I was repeatedly told how great I looked and that the changes made me look ten to fifteen years younger.

"What I wasn't prepared for were the other changes that started happening in my life. I was so interested in what I had learned that I found myself constantly studying others' faces for clues to their Energy Types and thinking about their behavior and personality tendencies and how that affected my relationships with them. I had some profound experiences in my work as a result of knowing my Energy Type and realizing how to better apply and use my gifts. I reconnected with parts of myself that I'd lost touch with through the ups and downs of life and felt more centered. I understood my husband, children, grandchildren, and friends in new ways. And as I fielded questions from many women who wondered how they could experience similar changes, I realized how passionate I was becoming about sharing the new knowledge and tools I'd gained with every woman who wanted to discover not only how to dress and look their best, but to know and love themselves more fully.

"Because you can't dress your truth until you know your truth, the Energy Profiling system challenges all of us to look deeply inside ourselves and remember who we really are and what we have to offer to the world so we can mirror that on the outside. It teaches us that there are many ways to move through life and to honor all those ways in ourselves and others. Sometimes it's uncomfortable and disconcerting, but it's worth the effort. When we know our truth, dressing to harmonize with our Energy Type and unique nature is satisfying because we are reflecting who we really are. For many of us, it's the first time we've been comfortable

saying to ourselves and the world, "This is the beautiful, gifted, amazing me!"

"A short nine-month journey has brought me to an amazing point in my life. I look and feel beautiful (despite my age!). I know and love who I am to a greater degree than before, and I am continuing to learn my life purposes and how to be. I have a new business that I know will continue to grow and bring me freedom, flexibility, and prosperity as I invite others to discover their true natures and transform their lives from the inside out. It's an unexpected place to be and I'm loving it!"

—LORI SQUIRES (TYPE 4^{SM} ENERGY), NEVADA

"I am 18 years old, and I was first introduced to Dressing Your Truth when I was 17… I could immediately see that I had a lot of TYPE 2^{SM} tendencies. I pay a lot of attention to detail—often too much attention. The object lesson they used was the building of a house. They said that the TYPE 2^{SM} [people] are the ones who ask all the detail questions: who, what, when, where, why, and how? That sounded exactly like me!

"As the instructors continued to describe each Energy Type, I saw more of me in the TYPE 2^{SM} and 4^{SM} Energies, and I also started to see my family members and friends in the other Energy Types. I began to understand why I think and act differently than my siblings, father, and friends and why my mom [who also expresses TYPE 2^{SM} Energy] and I are so similar. I also realized why my Mom would often pick out clothes for me and then end up wearing them more herself: because she would pick out TYPE 2^{SM}/1 clothes, which were too busy for the TYPE 2^{SM}/4 clothes I preferred!

"This Energy Profiling class opened up so many new vistas for me… Not only have I immensely enjoyed my new look, but I have also learned more about myself and my personality. I more fully understand why I am so attentive to detail while others around me couldn't care less. I understand why my siblings and parents deal with problems differently than I do. For instance, when my sister develops an opinion about something and someone contradicts her, she defends her point of view to the bitter end, insisting that she should always be right. This is not usually how I handle things, and I always wondered why she was like that. I didn't think I'd ever been that obnoxious when I was 13! After the Energy Profiling class, when we realized she is a 4, I understood why my sister acts like that—it's her energy! These and other examples have helped me develop better relationships with my family and the people around me. I just completed my first semester at college where I lived on campus with two roommates who are very different from me. One is a TYPE 1^{SM} Energy, the other is TYPE 3^{SM} Energy, so, so we each have our own personalities and our own methods in the way we do things. I even realized that our study habits are different. Whereas I can successfully study one subject for hours at a time, my roommates prefer to study little pieces at a time with small breaks in between.

"The things that I have learned have really helped me to understand who I am and accept myself and others and love others all the more because of it!"

—ARIELLE MYERS (TYPE 2^{SM} ENERGY), UTAH

PART

■ WHERE I CAME UP WITH ALL OF THIS!

WHERE I CAME UP WITH ALL OF THIS!

A COMMON QUESTION I AM ASKED IS, "Where did you come up with all of this?" Rather than keep you guessing or coming up with assumptions that are not accurate, I will answer that question— being true to my TYPE 3^{SM}/4 nature—get right to the point and tell it like it is! I have even added a lot more detail than is typical for me for those of you who want all the details.

I have been working in the field of Energy Psychology since 1994. As an author, energy therapist, and speaker, I have been very successful. I had a private practice for 13 years, seeing hundreds of personal clients as an energy therapist. I was not really out looking for something new to add to my profession. Creating such a successful private practice, seminar and Internet business, selling my home study courses, DVDs, CDs, and books while raising five children, kept my plate pretty full, even with my TYPE 3^{SM} Energy!

In 2004, a client of mine invited me to attend a small workshop put on by a woman by the name of Taylore Sinclaire, who owned a business called Illuminessensce. My friend told me a little about it, and it sounded intriguing. I happened to be in Phoenix, Arizona, doing a speaking engagement the same week Taylore was there doing a workshop, so I signed up. This one-day event briefly taught me that I was a Tone 3, according to her system, and that I would look my best if I wore more angles and textures and certain colors on my body. I was given a quick transformation along with a notebook to teach me more and a color fan to help me with future shopping. I was intrigued and could definitely see a difference in how I looked.

No background information was shared to explain what was Taylore assessed that made her declare me a Tone 3. I was told who I was without any insight into why that was. What was she looking at and measuring in me to determine that? I went on to attend a four-day event to learn more about the dressing system she taught and bits and pieces about being a Tone 3. In Taylore's system, in order to know what Tone you are, you had to either attend a live event or take a multiple choice test and submit it and a picture of yourself to be assessed by an Expert who then told you what Tone you are according to their system. Each profile cost $350. I went ahead and encouraged my other family members to be assessed, which my husband Jonathan and three of my five children and one son-in-law decided to do.

Of the five people who were assessed by this system, we learned (after I began to develop my own model) that two of the five had not been assessed correctly. My son Mark was assessed as a Tone 2 and my son-in-law Tony was assessed as a Tone 1. They are both classic textbook examples of TYPE 4^{SM} Energy Types. My son Mark was only 16 at the time and during those 6 months of thinking he was someone he was not, I can now see why his TYPE 4^{SM} tendencies became even more pronounced in his expression. He was not happy and felt very confused.

At the time, I truly felt this information had value and went on to host a four-day training, bringing in three Illuminessensce trainers to teach 24 women who had come from my marketing efforts to my internet database. That was in the fall of 2004. Following the Illuminessensce practice of assessing people and telling them their Tone, we had some interesting and emotional reactions. Let's just say not everyone was happy with the results! It was an expensive training in my opinion, with very little background information taught to be able to successfully duplicate the system to get personalized results.

With my secondary TYPE 4^{SM} Energy, I could see a lot of the flaws in it. It was what it was and if you are one of those original 24 women who came, I hope you will give me another chance with the system I have since created!

In my eagerness to help other people, I approached Taylore to see if there was a way to do some business together to help her get this information out there. We even approached her about selling us her business. Neither of those things were meant to happen, so they didn't. At this point, my client friend and I decided to pursue our own course with this information. That didn't work out either, so I was left to my own resources. I can't tell you how many times I have wanted to just throw in the towel on this information with the number of hurdles I have had to jump over in the process.

I had been told by the Illuminessensce people that they were the originators of this information and there was nothing else like it in the world. What happened next was very interesting because, with my secondary TYPE 4^{SM} Energy, I take people at their word and had no reason to question their claim.

Just a few months later, I was introduced to a Utah-based group called Human Art that was owned by a woman named Brooke Thornley. Another client who attended my somewhat disappointing first event had heard about this system and invited me to attend a one-day workshop they were offering in Ogden, Utah. I went and learned their take on how the body expresses movement, which determines which of the four groups you lead with. Their groups are called whitened, grayed, blackened, and saturated. The Human Art model is based more on principles of movement and how they relate to art. I quickly learned that Illuminessensce was not the only one with this kind of information. I also approached this group to investigate if there was an opportunity to help them with their business. They were not interested. They also made the claim that they were the originators of this kind of information and the only ones teaching it. Hmmm, something seemed fishy here!

Now this almost gets funny—if not miraculous! Within the next week, my mom, who attended my first event and learned the Illuminessensce approach, called me and shared, "I attended this course back in 1982 that taught similar information. I have a small bag of notes that I have kept in a canvas bag that has been hanging on my closet doorknob for all these years. Would you like me to send it to you?" My mom expresses TYPE 2^{SM} Energy, thank goodness, or I might not have had the most important piece I needed to give me the legal green light I needed to go ahead and create my own system.

All through this, I had been consulting my trademark and patent attorney, Grant Clayton, to make sure I kept myself in integrity and did not make any illegal choices since I was working with established systems and businesses. Grant told me the pre-existing art I found disputes the claims of Illuminessensce and Human Art being the originators of the concepts. This provided the solid ground I needed to move forward.

My mom sent me her canvas bag that had been untouched for 23 years and I laughed as I went through it. I discovered that the program my mom attended in 1982 was called Personal Style Consulting and they taught four groups that they called Bright, Soft, Rich, and Striking! My mom kept detailed notes about her experience with the program and what applied to her, but next to no information on how they came to their conclusions about your dominant group. Interestingly, my mom was not assessed properly in that system as well—they told her she was a Bright with a secondary Rich. In my system that would compare to dominant TYPE 1^{SM} Energy with secondary TYPE 3^{SM} Energy, but in the Energy Profiling model, she expresses dominant TYPE 2^{SM} Energy through and through. Thank heaven she kept a canvas bag hanging on a closet door for 23 years!

Her very TYPE 2^{SM} behavior was the missing link that made it possible for me to share this information with you!

In our research, we have not been able to find any existing information that Personal Style Consulting is still in business. But what my mom had saved for all these years supported the fact that there is no single original system out there. Who knows where it all started?

I just knew that there was yet to be a model created that supported people in assessing themselves. This model would teach the foundation of what was the compelling force behind the four Energy Types, which match movement with the harmonious design elements to wear on the body.

So from 2005 to 2009, that is what I developed. Many of my insights have been directly revealed to me from Spirit. I am deeply grateful that the three other existing programs I have mentioned gave me a window of awareness of what this is all about. Through it all, I hope that what I have created is of great value to you and that my efforts and results makes a lasting impression on improving the quality of your life.

WHAT I LEARNED FROM MY HOME LABORATORY

I have had the great benefit of living in a home laboratory ever since I started to develop this information. Our family is currently composed of the following dominant Energy Types:

- TYPE 1^{SM} Energy—Jenny (oldest child), Mario (fifth and youngest child), Jaleah (Mark's wife)

- TYPE 2^{SM} Energy—Jonathan (my husband), Chris (second child), Anne (third child), Neal (Jenny and Tony's son)

- TYPE 3^{SM} Energy—Carol (me), Tanner (Anne's husband), Sarah (Chris' wife), Joseph (Jenny and Tony's son), Katie Claire (Anne and Tanner's daughter)

- TYPE 4^{SM} Energy—Tony (Jenny's husband), Mark (fourth child), Seth (Jenny and Tony's son)

I love it! We have such fun with each other with next to no conflict in our relationships now that we understand each other better. I have learned a tremendous amount about each of the four Energy Types in people from my home laboratory of family members. To add to my learning, I decided to interview each family member and asked them the following questions:

"How has knowing your dominant Energy Type made a difference in the overall quality of your life and your relationships?"

"What is something you judged as negative about yourself that you now accept as a gift?"

"How has knowing your gifts made a difference in your life experience and the understanding of who you are?"

What resulted from those questions were some very enjoyable and incredible conversations. The notes I took from what I was learning gave me a lot of insights that I was able to include in this book. I am grateful that all the members of my family have been so open and willing to share their stories. We each understand that what we have been given is so valuable that we are eager to share our everyday experiences to help others live their truth and create more harmonious relationships.

PART 7

■ A Parting Story

A Parting Story

BEFORE I CONCLUDE THE BOOK, I want to share a story. You may have heard of Paul Potts. He won the first *Britain's Got Talent* competition in 2007. A salesman for Car Phone Warehouse from Cardiff, Wales, he utterly shocked skeptical judges Piers Morgan, Amanda Holden, and Simon Cowell—and brought the house to their feet—with a stunning performance of "Nessun Dorma," an aria from Puccini's *Turandot*. Paul's winning performance has been viewed by hundreds of millions of people worldwide.

Paul expresses TYPE 2^{SM} Energy, as evidenced by his oval face and soft demeanor. He was self-effacing about his voice talent, saw himself as flawed and weak, and showed a major lack of self-confidence. He spent much of his life feeling insignificant, just blending into the background.

Bullied as a child, Paul lacked self-esteem, but a deep sensitivity also gave him the ability to present his tenor voice with great tenderness. Though he doubted he could make it professionally, he was so driven by his own hidden talent that he had to give *Britain's Got Talent* a try.

Paul was once told that he was a natural salesman. "But," he explains in his official online biography, "I knew I wasn't. When I was selling, I always felt like I was putting on an act. When I sang, that's when I felt like I was myself—the real me."

Paul knew who he was deep down, but it wasn't until his performance before Piers, Amanda, and Simon that he came to share his real self. When he came forward acknowledging his gifts and talents—and validating himself with them—he came into his own power. Shortly after his win, he recorded his first album, which rocketed to #1 in its category on charts across the world, and he spent the next year touring the globe.

Consider the effect he had on the judges. By demonstrating and living his gift, he brings them into a rare moment of harmony as all the energies merge and unite.

The judge Amanda expresses TYPE 1^{SM} Energy. You'll notice her apple cheeks and high forehead. She was moved to tears by Paul's singing, which is an example of a rapid shift. With her TYPE 1^{SM} Energy, it's her role to lift up those around her. She lifted the audience and Paul with her cheery and uplifting take on Paul's performance.

Piers expresses TYPE 3^{SM} Energy. Can you see the angles in his face? When you watch the video of Paul's first round performance, you'll notice Piers' instant— perhaps impatient—skepticism when Paul announces that he'll be singing opera. But Piers comes full circle when he sees the results. He was delighted with the performance and didn't mince words.

Simon, with his TYPE 4^{SM} Energy, was precise and direct in his appraisal when he said, "You were absolutely a breath of fresh air." High praise from someone who sees in black and white.

When Paul came into balance with who he really was, other energies in his presence came into balance as well. That's the ideal: to come into balance with ourselves and with those around us. Paul, Piers, Amanda, and Simon all did it without knowing about their own Energy Types, but you are now better equipped.

Everyone's combination of Energy Types is perfect. When you add up the numbers 1, 2, 3, and 4, they equal 10! Everyone gets to be their own perfect 10 in their own unique and beautiful way.

You should well know your own Energy Type by now. Use this knowledge to balance and harmonize your life, and help others to do so, too. That's why I have shared this gift with you. Use it! Bless your own life and the lives of everyone around you. God bless you in your journey!

PART

■ ADDITIONAL RESOURCES: MORE SUPPORT
FOR KNOWING AND LIVING YOUR TRUE
NATURE

More Support for Knowing and Living Your True Nature

AS I MENTIONED IN THE FIRST PART OF THIS BOOK, I created three resources to help you learn more about your Energy Type. These same three resources will help you if you need more support in knowing and living your true nature!

They are:

1. This book
2. The Energy Profiling website: www.myenergyprofile.com
3. The Carol Blog: www.thecarolblog.com

Here is how you can make the most of each of these resources:

THIS BOOK

It's Just My Nature! is a book that you will get more and more value from if you read it more than once. As you become aware of your Energy Type, you will begin a self-awareness journey that will naturally unfold itself to you. When you return to the book to read about your dominant Energy Type, new things will stand out for you, along with more inspiration and revelations about your true nature. As you read about the other dominant Energy Types, you will have the same experience in understanding the people in your life. I encourage you to share this book with people you are involved with in relationships. You will find that as their understanding grows, they will support you, and you all will have a more expanded awareness, enabling you to honor each others' gifts.

THE ENERGY PROFILING WEBSITE

At the Energy Profiling website, you will find a number of valuable resources to help you live your true nature. We built this website to complement this book. At www.myenergyprofile.com, you can take the Energy Profiling assessment online training to more fully understand your true nature. This interactive learning experience uses video, audio, and Flash technology to make your Energy Profiling learning experience a more multi-sensory experience, as we are able to include a wide range of images, pictures, and visuals that are not available in this book.

Other features of the online Energy Profiling learning experience include images of facial features and facial characteristics described in each of the Energy Type sections of this book. Body Profiling is one of the most telling assessments in learning your dominant Energy Type, so it will help you to see what we mean when we say TYPE 1^{SM} Energy expresses as circles in their facial features, like apple cheeks! Seeing the images of different facial features will help you become more skilled with the Body Profiling assessment tools of the Energy Profiling system.

THE CAROL BLOG

When learning about Energy Types, many people find out that they have not been living true to their nature throughout their lives. Discovering this is a big relief, but can also bring up some emotional discomfort. It is my goal on The Carol Blog to continue to offer support in helping you live your truth through the many written and video posts that go up weekly. You will find support in determining your Energy Type on the blog, as well as receive ongoing support for helping you live true to your nature. We have posted content to help you improve your relationships, experience better health, make more money, succeed in your career, and more—all true to your nature. You can find several of the resources mentioned throughout this book:

- The Relationships Guide: Get practical relationship tips for you and your partner's particular combination of Energy Types.

- Achieve optimum health: Lose weight, end chronic pain, and resolve body imbalances by checking the Health section of the blog.

- Make more money: Under the Money section of the blog, you will find helpful resources for improving your career and attracting more money.

The Carol Blog is a fun and entertaining resource to help you know and live true to your nature!

In addition to those resources to help you learn your Energy Type, I have created several other online resources, programs, and books to support you in living true to your nature. Explore and enjoy whichever resources feel most important to you right now.

CAROL TUTTLE HEALING CENTER

If you are like many adults, discovering your Energy Type can bring up emotional issues or negative judgments you're still holding onto from the past. As an energy therapist, I have supported people worldwide in learning energy healing techniques to clear emotional baggage, childhood issues, or other limiting beliefs. Learn these techniques with me online at youremotionalhealing.com

REMEMBERING WHOLENESS

My first book is a handbook for thriving that helps you tap into the power you have to create the life you want. The principles in it apply to all Energy Types. Get your copy at caroltuttle.com

THE CHILD WHISPERER

When you know your Energy Type and your child's Energy Type, suddenly the typical parent-child struggles take on a whole new look. I take that shift a step further in my book, *The Child Whisperer*, with the intent to make those struggles completely disappear. If you have children, work with children, know children, or were a child yourself, this book will be valuable for you.

Many of the negative judgments you carry about yourself and your Energy Type took root in your childhood. The good news is that our children don't have to experience the same wounds that we did as children. When we identify our children's dominant Energy Type, we can customize our parenting to support their true nature. Children who are parented according to The Child Whisperer model are happier, successful, and more cooperative.

Earlier in this book, I mentioned a video series that complements the book in identifying your child's Energy Type. Find the book and profiling videos at thechildwhisperer.com

DRESSING YOUR TRUTH FOR WOMEN AND MEN

As you discovered in this book, your Type of energy shows up in your features and your body's natural movement. In other words, your appearance is inseparably linked to your Energy Type. A very important, supportive next step in living your true nature is learning to dress true to your Energy Type. When you wear clothes that honor your Energy Type's natural quality and movement, you naturally feel more comfortable in your own skin and you look great.

That's the reason I created online learning courses to teach both women and men how to dress according to their Energy Type. These online programs teach you how to honor your true nature in what you put on your body. When you do, your outward expression matches your inner self, and you will naturally feel more confident, comfortable, and empowered to move through life true to your unique energy.

ONLINE EXPERIENCE FOR WOMEN

The Dressing Your Truth online experience offers a woman hours of personal beauty training in the comfort of her own home via the internet. Our state-of-the-art online learning courses, along with our other resources, include:

1. Your very own Dressing Your Truth online course for your Type of beauty. The course teaches you which clothes, jewelry, makeup, hairstyle and skin care are perfect for you.
2. Regular Club Nights—broadcast online—feature a variety of topics to continue to support you in Dressing Your Truth.
3. Club Nights Video Vault allows you access to recordings of previous Club Nights.
4. Images of hairstyles and outfits will give you plenty of ideas for maximizing your Type of beauty.
5. Community Forums are available where you can support—and receive support from—other women with your Type of beauty.

The Dressing Your Truth experience also includes my book, *Dressing Your Truth—Discover Your Type of Beauty*. This book discusses how we blame ourselves for not looking and feeling great in the clothes we own, only to discover that we've been using the wrong measuring stick! It's not us—it is the system that has failed us.

The Dressing Your Truth world is a lot of fun for me because I get to offer so many options to women to support them in looking beautiful and feeling confident. To see the current resources we're offering in our salon, store, and website, visit dressingyourtruth.com.

ONLINE EXPERIENCE FOR MEN

Our customized style course supports men in experiencing more success and confidence in all areas of their life—starting with something as simple as their wardrobe. The online resources we created help you align your Energy Type's natural gifts to achieve what you want most in life. We also walk you through components of casual and professional style that are best for your Energy Type, giving you an easy formula to look great every day.

All the men in our company dress according to their Energy Type. This practice supports them in consistently working in a manner that's true to them, and it also serves as a visual reminder for their coworkers of what to expect from them. I truly believe that the way all of our employees—men and women—honor themselves in the way they dress is one of the reasons our company culture is so supportive.

Find the Dressing Your Truth online course for men at dressingyourtruth.com/men

May you take advantage of all the support you need as you live your truth.

ABOUT THE AUTHOR

CAROL TUTTLE IS A CATALYST for change who improves the quality of our lives. She has worked in the field of Energy Therapy for over a decade and a half in the pursuit of helping others live their truth. She is a best-selling author, radio show host, speaker, and successful business woman. As the creator and founder of both the Energy Profiling and Dressing Your Truth programs, she offers you the very finest of her work yet. Having worked in the self-help and self-realization field for most of her career, she has experienced the myriad of tools and systems we resource to assist us in discovering and living our truth. She shares, "Hands down, the Energy Profiling and Dressing Your Truth systems are the most remarkable resources I have ever had the opportunity to teach. I continue to marvel at the impact this information has on a person. It seems to speak to a deep, innate sense of truth within us that allows people to live their authentic self effortlessly. I am forever grateful to be the voice that shares this important information with the world. Thank you for letting me play this role in your life. God bless you." —*Carol Tuttle*

Carol is married to Jonathan Tuttle. They are the parents of five children and they reside in Draper, Utah, a suburb of Salt Lake City. For more information about Carol and her body of work, please visit www.thecarolblog.com.